D1246292

FIND *your* THING.

ESCAPE MONOTONY
IN YOUR **MID-20'S**
& **DO WORK**
THAT MATTERS

LISA ZELENAK

To the people that inspire me...
challenge me...
& call me out on the daily...

. . .

Mom & Dad

(You always showed me I could do anything;
you always gave me the space to do my thing)

. . .

Ange

(My inspiration & an inspiration to so many
people that want to Find Their Thing)

. . .

Ryan Cooper,

Gary Williams,

Taylor Funk,

Crystal Kaminski

(You are the reason I finished this book...and well, also the reason I almost
never finished because you continue to inspire me with new content daily)

. . .

Aaron Donaghy

(Looking back, I finally realized you taught me
all of this, what, 14 years ago?)

. . .

Chandler Bolt & Self Publishing School

(Literally would not have published without you.)

PURPOSE:

INTRODUCTION.

SO ... YOU WANT TO CHANGE THE WORLD, BUT YOU DON'T KNOW YOUR *THING?*

You know there is more to life,
but you have no idea how to find it.

You have been tirelessly looking, but left feeling empty.

Am I missing something?
How do I find purpose?
Do I even have purpose?

You want to impact people,
you want to make BIG things happen in the world,
but you feel like you're watching life slip away.

"What is my purpose?
What am I called to do?
How can I impact others to gain back my sense of fulfillment?
Because I *hate* feeling this way."

So many questions.
And no answers.
No clarity.

You feel like something is missing inside of you.

If you could just *Find Your Thing*,
Everything would be better.
You're right, you are missing something.
The hole in your heart is robbing you of your joy and your satisfaction.

In fact, most pieces in life root back to this void.
When you are frustrated and can't even explain why,
You would give anything to fill it.

This book will reveal one simple shift in your approach that you need.
If you give me permission to show you, this simple shift will finally give you your
clarity — clarity that is not fleeting. It will not disappear in a matter of days or
years. It will ignite you in a new way and bring you to a new level of fulfillment.

Skeptical?
I hear you.
I remember I wouldn't even look at an article, let alone an entire book that said
"How to find your purpose" or "5 ways to get to your purpose in 5 minutes." I
had already read them all, or at least I was convinced that there was nothing new
I didn't try. If there was in fact a magical solution I would have already heard
about it.

But trust me.
If you're looking for answers, there's no harm in trying.
THIS is exactly what worked for me.
And it's worked for many other people I've personally coached over the past five
years. People that felt lost and looking for purpose, but left saying,
"This is exactly what I needed."
"Lisa, you're a wizard."
*"Thank you. Seriously, thank you. This has impacted my career, my marriage, and how
excited I am about life."*
(Apparently I learned a thing or two when I got my Master's Degree in Human
Services Counseling/Life Coaching.)

By the end of this book, all of the questions that you can't seem to find the
answer to ...
     What job do I want?

Where do I want to work?

What is my passion?

What am I good at?

What is my next adventure?

Should I move to New York?

Should I go back to school?

Should I start a blog?

Should I drop everything and leave my job?

will suddenly have answers.

This book will show you the clarity you've been dying for.

All can be possible in less than a week if you read 20 minutes a day. ;)

But...

If you want to...

you can wait.

You can wait another 5 years.

Continuing to try your way, knowing that "It will come one day."

But don't be the reason you are lost.

Don't be the one that's too prideful to seek out help.

Don't be the one that's too lazy to change your path.

And please don't be the one that is too busy to read a short book that can alter the rest of your life.

Make the decision right now to invest in yourself and in your future.

Make the decision to *Find Your Thing*.

SECTION 1

THE PROBLEM.

CHAPTER 1

YES, YOU CAN SKIP THIS CHAPTER.

I GET IT.

You're already frustrated after having spent time trying to *Find Your Thing**

  *your purpose, your calling, your next step

with no real breakthrough. Instead of wasting your time with a Chapter One, let's get right to the point.

Feel liberated and jump right into Chapter Two.

See, you're already well on your way to *Find Your Thing*.

IF YOU WANT TO READ QUICKLY:

Read all of the bold text and anything different than the body text. You'll get the jist of the book. But consider this, if you move quickly, that may be the reason why you haven't yet found your thing.

CHAPTER 2

YOU ARE SOLVING THE WRONG PROBLEM.

SO YOU WANT TO *FIND YOUR THING*?

Most books on purpose start out asking you questions like:

> *"What do you enjoy?"*
> *"What are you passionate about?"*
> *"What do you like to do for fun?"*

Not this book.

My bet is you've already asked yourself these questions, only leaving frustrated and without a solid answer. **Instead of starting with what you like, this book starts with what you hate.**

It's time to cut to the heart of what matters most by beginning with your pain.

When you think back to high school, what subject did you hate most?

It's never been proven, but I'm certain the majority of people would say they hate math.

Whether you like math or you can barely understand the difference between sine and cosine, there is one thing that was always frustrating during the days of math class.

Do you remember that moment? That moment when you came into class so happy because you finished your 100 problems of homework, only to find out ... your teacher told you to do the odd problems, and you did all of the evens.

Man, what a terrible feeling. A complete waste. You spent time and energy investing in the problems that didn't even matter. Hard problems too, the answers to the even problems aren't even in the back of the book.

While your math days may be behind you, your predisposition to solving the wrong problem may not be.

> *What's my thing?*
> *Do I even have a thing?*
> *Will I ever have a thing?*

If you are asking these questions, it's likely you are already sitting in dissatisfaction and drowning in frustration. Some of you are beyond just questioning purpose and already on the border of feeling defeated.

> *Should I switch jobs?*
> *Do I need to go back to school?*
> *What's next for me?*

Many people are losing sleep each night, tirelessly wondering, "Is there something out there that will be more fulfilling?"

What if the reason you can't Find Your Thing is that you are solving the wrong problem?

You may see the problem, but there is almost always something deeper going on. Did you ever think to find out where the problem originated? The pain that you've always identified as "lack of purpose" might be making the real issue.

Here's a new approach to the problem you've been wrestling with for what could be a week, a month, or maybe even years.

If you're desperately trying to *Find Your Thing*, the best place to start is by understanding where your pain originated.

GET CRYSTAL CLEAR ON THE PAIN.

Think of the last time you had a headache. (If you haven't had a headache, then you are a super human and you can stop reading this book.)

When you get a headache, what do you do? Most people take a couple of Advil and call it a day. While you can treat the symptoms of a headache with a pain pill, it rarely does anything to solve the real problem. There is likely a deeper issue.

Why do you have a headache in the first place? Stress? Nerve pain? Problems with your spinal alignment?

Many issues in society grow from us not getting directly to the root of the problem. It is easy to jump in and start solving your problems without having first assessed the core of the issue. When you don't get to the root of the problem, how can you expect to accurately solve it?

PERCEIVED PROBLEM VS. ROOT ISSUE.

Are you solving the wrong problem in your relationships?
Your boyfriend has been slow to respond to your text messages and phone calls, and denied almost all of your attempts to spend time together. You're frustrated, asking, "Why aren't you spending time with me?" "Was it something that I did?"

Meanwhile, he is under a lot pressure at work, unsure how to process, and exhausted by the time he gets home. While you might have had the assumption that his behavior was in response to something you did, in reality his problem has nothing to do with you.

In order to have a solution, you have to identify the actual problem.
Are you solving the wrong problem in the most basic areas of life?
While standing in line at the grocery store, you start getting annoyed with your family, asking, "Why do I always have to get us groceries?"
Meanwhile, you internally feel like you have nothing good going for you in life

right now. **Nothing can move forward when you are solving the wrong problem.**

Your greatest likelihood to solve any problem is uncovering the true root. Purpose is no different.

As you dive in to *Find Your Thing*, look to the internal root of the problem to see what is really going on.

Without awareness of what is happening beneath the surface, you run the risk of spending time and energy solving the wrong problem. Worse, if you continue solving the wrong problem, you'll find yourself spiraling down to rock bottom.

To avoid rock bottom, you need to develop true self awareness.

Awareness doesn't come easily because most of us were never taught how to become aware. We grew up learning how to tie our shoes and write the alphabet, but before we knew it, we had been in school for 12 years straight with few, if any, opportunities on how to become more self-aware.
There is no wonder we become paralyzed when it comes time to decide our college major or choose our first job. We have never really been set up to know who we are, let alone who we want to be.

By the time you hit the real world, lack of awareness and understanding of who you are will often surface as "What's my purpose?" or "What's my thing?"

This uncertainty can create a frustrating state of mind where your expectations and reality do not align, leaving you feeling defeated. Simply putting off the question does not make it go away. Even into middle age and retirement, lack of awareness is still present and painful. Reflecting on life, it can be overwhelming to think: Who am I? What do I want to be? What do I want to do with my life?

Living in the fullness of life is dependent on awareness. Whichever stage of life you're in now, it is crucial to learn awareness because without it, the constant questioning of "Why am I not living a fulfilled life?" will not go away.

What is the reason you lack self-awareness?

There are two reasons why most people lack awareness:

1. People are not taught how to be become self-aware. How can you become aware when you aren't given the tools?

2. Awareness is uncomfortable. Humans have an overwhelming desire for comfort, much more than they desire awareness. It is easier to live in comfort than it is to face the painful truth that comes from awareness.

LACK OF AWARENESS CAN PARALYZE YOU.

Without awareness, how can you expect to understand what you are looking for?

Without understanding what you are looking for, how can you expect to find it?

You might be thinking:

"Trust me, I am aware. If my purpose was already here, I would have seen it."

After multiple studies, Tasha Eurich concluded, "95% of people think they are self-aware, but only 10-15% truly are [self aware]." Many people think they are self-aware, but simply don't realize there is more truth they are missing. "You don't know what you don't know."

Let me guess, you think you're in the 10 percent? (Great, then you know the value of awareness and probably crave an in-depth understanding.)

The illusion is that if you are an incredibly gifted individual, you often think you have life figured out and that you don't need awareness. I'm here to tell you I was top of my class, an athlete, a world traveler, homecoming queen of 30,000 people at my university and I still lacked awareness. It's not about being gifted. It's about identifying a deeper level of who you are.

Even after I had my first major encounter with awareness, which you will soon read about, I discovered I could repeat this process indefinitely for the rest of my life. So, if you think you don't need awareness, if you think you don't need this process, you're wrong. There is no limit to the growth and awareness that you can have.

The truth is, even the things that seem so obvious, the things you would swear by, are easy to miss without awareness. My pastor, Erwin McManus, once described this as the Tom Brady Effect. Many people can recognize good football. (If you can't tell the difference between the defense and the offense, think of an example in your life where you can recognize talent.) Most people that watch Tom Brady can tell he is a good football player. Many would even say Brady is the greatest player of all time. Every team wants a Tom Brady. Coaches, players, and fans will ask, "Why can't we have a Tom Brady?" The funny thing is, every team could have had a Tom Brady. Every team passed Brady up in the 2000 NFL draft. Even the Patriots passed Tom Brady up multiple times before finally grabbing him in the sixth round. The talent was in front of every coach, but the coaches didn't have the eyes to see. The coaches didn't posses the full awareness to see Tom Brady's skill and capability.

Awareness makes all the difference.

. . . .

Many have jumped from job to job, moved halfway across the world to a beautiful city, or started a new endeavor, thinking that would finally solve the problem. They later find themselves back at square one, looking for a new answer.

On the way to awareness, you'll go through the things you hate. There will be a lot of pain involved before you get to the things you value. But if you stick around and follow the process, the answer to your question of "What's my thing?" will become clear.

This book is a combination of reading your mind and translating the language of purpose. That is how you get to the core—the core of what matters most.

Deeper awareness = Deeper understanding of purpose

EVEN IF YOU ONLY GET THIS:

- One of the biggest mistakes people make in life is that they spend time and energy solving the wrong problem in relationships, in business, and when it comes to finding purpose.

- Before you jump in with two feet looking to get a quick answer to *Find Your Thing*, make sure you are solving for the *right* thing.

- There is often a deeper issue that you miss simply because you lack awareness about who you are. You lack awareness of your fears and your values.

> *Why it matters to Find Your Thing*
  Your purpose will be clear when you have the awareness.

IF YOU STOP READING NOW,
YOU'LL MISS THIS:

" *There are these two young fish swimming along, and they happen to meet an older fish swimming the other way, who nods at them and says, 'Morning, boys, how's the water?' And the two young fish swim on for a bit, and then eventually one of them looks over at the other and goes, 'What the hell is water?'* "

DAVID FOSTER WALLACE

There are many things you are surrounded by on a daily basis that although they influence every aspect of our lives, you lack awareness of their existence.

The next chapter will dive into something, some things, that have influenced you for years, most likely without your knowledge or permission.

Without your understanding, these can suffocate you. They can limit what you believe you are capable of achieving. These can distract you from pursuing what you really want in life and can leave you feeling horrible because you don't know your thing. Just like a fish can be surrounded by water without full awareness of what it is, humans are surrounded by something that influences the way they live.

CHAPTER 3

HOW I BECAME AWARE.

I REMEMBER THE MOMENT I BECAME AWARE.
It started on a beach in Maui when I was learning how to surf. For most of my life, learning new things came relatively easy to me. A few years previously in California, I went surfing and I remember doing pretty well.

Despite doing well at surfing in the past, this time I was struggling to get up on the surfboard. The waves just weren't going my way. After about an hour, I managed to stand up only a few times. It felt and looked pretty pathetic because even when I finally did stand up on the surfboard, it wasn't anything impressive.

I was getting frustrated with myself.

At the time I didn't understand my frustration. I thought I was just mad that I couldn't get up on a surfboard. That seemed normal; who doesn't like to be good at things? **I didn't realize there was a deeper issue I'd been ignoring.**

After yet another failed attempt, I started swimming over to get back in the surf line to try again. As I was swimming over, I looked up and happened to be right next to a *real* surfer. My instructor explained to us earlier that he was the best on the island. This remarkable surfer was casually sitting on a paddle board. (That's right he was so good, he didn't even need a surfboard to surf.) His dog was even more casually perched up on the front of the board. The surfer seemed like he didn't have a care in the world as he waited patiently for the next good wave.

Something led me to call out to him.

"Hey! I give you props for being able to surf so well! I can't even get up on the board."

The surfer looked over in my direction. His eyes met mine and in the calm voice of your stereotypical surfing type, he responded, *"I'm sure you're better than me at a lot of things."*

Right then it hit me.

His seemingly meaningless 11 words hit me like a tidal wave.

A rush of thoughts came flooding through my mind.

It all made sense. *This* was dominating my life.
Unwritten Rules.
Unwritten Rules were dominating my life.
I never knew these "rules" existed until that moment in the ocean.
If I can't get up on the surfboard, then I am a failure.

Before that moment, I had sold my soul.
Part of my worth was being determined by whether or not I could get up on a surfboard. And not *just* a surfboard. The reality is that my value was being put into how long I could stand up on something that was nothing more than a painted piece of training foam. That seemed a little ridiculous.
Because it was ridiculous.
It *is* ridiculous.

Why should the value of who I am be determined by something external?

The surfer was right. Yes, I probably *was* better than him at other things. But really, what did it matter?
Why does it matter?
Why does it matter if I am good at surfing?
Why does it matter if I am better than him at other skills like connecting with strangers?

In the weeks that followed this moment, my mind continued to race. More and more I began to notice just how much my worth as a human was dictated by Unwritten Rules.

I subconsciously allowed Unwritten Rules to define who I was, without my awareness, let alone my permission.

Unwritten Rule:

Defining identity* based on external circumstances.

*Identity:

Belief about who you are.

Your beliefs proceed your actions. Therefore, what you believe about who you are is powerful.

You may know Unwritten Rules by other names — assumed expectations, the voice in your head, the overwhelming weight of the general consensus of society. These rules were dictating my definition of success. These rules told me what made me significant and therefore had control of almost every aspect of my life.

At the time I learned this lesson, my job did not look like the average person's "career." I wasn't working a conventional 40 hour work week, and I definitely did not get paid much. As a result, the Unwritten Rules in my head told me I was less valuable and I believed them.

Rules had power over my life.

If a rule exists in your life, you have given it power and authority over you. You are no longer in control of who you believe you are.

I'll show you in the simplest form. Finish this sentence:

If you work at McDonald's, then you are _____.

The way you finish that sentence will give insight to one of your rules and insight to your deep rooted beliefs.

If you work at McDonald's, then you are a *loser.*
If you work at McDonald's, then you are *employed.*
How you finish the statement matters.

Maybe you'll never work at McDonalds, you couldn't care less about surfing, and you are well paid for the work you do. Unwritten Rules are still present in your life.

The danger comes when you don't see how Unwritten Rules have control over your choices.

When I first experienced my Unwritten Rules in Hawaii, I considered myself to be smart and emotionally strong. Despite having high emotional intelligence, I was still held back by the belief that if you can't surf, then you are *less.* **My subconscious value system was crushing me. This value system had been crushing me for years, I was just never aware.**

Unwritten Rules are the standard for how you define personal value.
Your rules define how you place value on yourself and others.

[*IF* EXTERNAL EVENT ,
THEN IDENTITY*.]

If you leave right at 5 p.m., you are not a hard worker.
If your house is a mess, then you're a horrible mother.
If you didn't go to college, then you're a failure.

In your job, rules exists.
In your family, rules exists.
In your closest relationship, rules exists.
In your generation, rules exists.
In your friend group, rules exists.
In your culture, rules exists.
In your religion, rules exists.

DO I NEED TO WRITE DOWN MY RULES?

Find one Unwritten Rule in your life before the end of this chapter.
(For now, make mental notes of what Unwritten Rules appear in your life.)

Although you're the author of your rules, others are the source. While I wrote the rule that I am less for not being able to surf, this Unwritten Rule came from my parents' high expectations.

As soon as you were born, other people were already dictating to you how you should feel about yourself. Parents, teachers, strangers, and as you grew up, siblings, friends, and significant others. **Rules aren't the same for everyone.** Rules are shaped by your unique surroundings.

Some rules are society's ever present judgement resting on your shoulders. Other rules have come from your pursuit to resist society's ever present judgement.

Your rules are specific to you. There isn't one societal expectation of all. Unwritten Rules link to your specific desires, and therefore they don't lie. If you examine them, they will show you your truth. They show you how you see the world. They show you your deepest values because your desires are rooted in your Unwritten Rules.

Unwritten Rules influence your personal value system. Your beliefs about who you are influence your decisions.

Your decisions create your reality, therefore, your rules cannot be ignored. There is too much at stake. Rules are likely limiting you from experiencing the fullness of your potential. How do I know? The danger is in the external. Unwritten Rules mean that your internal value can rise or fall based on external events. That is dangerous.

Finish this sentence:
If I don't know my purpose, then I am _____.
The way you finish this statement is again insight to one of your rules and values.
If I don't know my purpose then I am a failure.
OR

If I don't know my purpose then I am on the verge of something great.

Do you see how your external rules define your internal value? Rules can determine your definition of success, your level of significance, and how you feel about your worth. Unwritten Rules will give you awareness at the deeper level you need.

Before you leave this chapter — *Every human being has a few core rules that dictate their life.* What are some of the personal rules you've noticed that are limiting you?

When people first see their rules, there are usually two responses:

1. **Ignore them.**

   It seems logical, right? Ignorance is often bliss, especially when it comes to self-awareness. Self-awareness of any kind can be overwhelming.

2. **Resist them and begin to try to break them.**

   Rules often hold us back from becoming who you want to be. The immediate desire is often to break your rules for the sake of knowing that they are not holding you back anymore. While I am all for breaking the rules, (and this book will help you with that if you choose later on) fighting furiously to solve the problem is not always the immediate answer. Just because you are swinging an axe does not mean you know where to hit. While you may try to break your rules, they will likely resurface if you don't get to the core.

You can ignore or run from your rules, but you will still be chained to them.

The power is in understanding your rules. To free yourself from rules for good, you must first understand them. Unwritten Rules govern your thought patterns and your actions. They influence what you say and how you say it. They even influence how you spend your time and who you spend your time with. The awareness that comes from diving deeper into your rules is the same awareness you will need to see purpose.

[*IF* YOU UNDERSTAND YOUR RULES,

THEN YOU'LL BE ABLE TO SEE YOUR PURPOSE.]

Your rules get to the core of what matters. When you understand the core of what matters to you, you will become closer to finding your purpose. There, you will *Find Your Thing.*

DO NOT MOVE ON FROM THIS CHAPTER UNTIL YOU
WRITE OUT ONE UNWRITTEN RULE IN YOUR LIFE:

IF _____ , THEN _____ .
       (EXTERNAL EVENT)   (IDENTITY)

EVEN IF YOU ONLY GET THIS:

- Unwritten Rules exist in your life.
  If I can't surf, then I'm a failure.
  If I work at McDonalds, then I'm a loser.

- Rules reflect your unique value system. They define how you place value on yourself and others.

- Unwritten Rules can be dangerous because your external events are defining your identity. Identity = what you believe about yourself.

> **Why it matters to Find Your Thing**
  When you become aware of your rules, you'll have one of the quickest tools to get to the depths of what matters most to you. When you understand the core of what matters to you, there you will
  Find Your Thing.

IF YOU STOP READING NOW,
YOU'LL MISS THIS:

Picture yourself running down the stairs in a hurry. Before you get to the bottom of the stairs, you hit your leg on the staircase. Ouch. It hurt but you continue with your day. Pretty soon you realize the "one time bruise" is the gift that keeps on giving. Later in the day, you're a little careless and you nail your bruise on a coworker's desk. You let out an unprofessional, "Son of a!..." and then you manage to maintain composure in front of your peers. Your bruise is directly connected to a previous source of pain that had an external cause.

In a similar way, our internal "bruise" has an external cause that can only be healed by protecting it from further damage. Both the external and internal bruises need to be sheltered from continuous harm.

The pain you experience from your bruise is like the pain you experience with your Unwritten Rules. They cause you pain one time and continue to cause you more pain over and over again. The question is - how long will you let them hurt you?

Your triggers (external events) flare up your internal pain. Good news: There are ways to avoid the inflammation. The first step is understanding your triggers. Understanding what brings on your pain will allow you to rid yourself of it.

CHAPTER 4

TRIGGERED.

WHEN YOU SEE SOMEONE THAT IS ABSOLUTELY *TERRIBLE* AT PARALLEL PARKING, HOW DO YOU REACT?

You know that person.

You see an open spot on the street and the car in front of you slows to a stop. He puts his blinker on to attempt one of the most socially risky endeavors known to man. He can single-handedly win or lose the approval of all those in proximity. He reverses into the spot but realizes he cut the wheel too tightly. He resets and you cringe as he narrowly misses the sports car in front of him. He tries again and abruptly hits the curb, as you look into the rear-view mirror and see four, five, now six cars behind you. His passenger is sinking in her seat as she becomes aware of people staring. He tries again thinking a victory has been secured but realizes he is still halfway in the street. So instead of enduring this humiliation, he speeds off pretending that he didn't want the spot anyway.

Maybe this is you. Maybe you are terrible at parallel parking. Regardless of whether or not you, can parallel park, how do you respond to someone who is terrible at parallel parking? Do you point and laugh? Do you roll your eyes? Do you empathize with them, knowing that you also aren't perfect at parallel parking every time?

The way you see people who can't parallel park says a lot about how you see yourself. If you shame people who cannot parallel park, it is likely that you feel ashamed when *you* cannot parallel park.

Do you feel internal pain when you can't parallel park?
This is called a trigger.

Trigger:
Experience of internal pain due to external circumstances.

You know that feeling when something happens, then all of a sudden you feel bad about who you are? You feel physical pain from your internal discomfort.
Like 1,000 pounds of weight on your chest…
Like you've been hit in the stomach and are feeling queasy …
Like your shoulders are heavy, and you want to run and hide under your covers, away from the world…
The pain might be new or maybe you've been carrying this weight for a while now.
Every person feels the discomfort in their own way.
Whatever it physically feels like for you, this is how you know you've landed on the first part of your Unwritten Rule — your trigger.

Unwritten Rules have two parts:
Trigger + Pain
   If *[Trigger]* then *[Pain]*.
   If I can't get up on the surfboard, then [Pain]
   If I can't parallel park, then [Pain]

If my friends come over and my house is a mess…
If I lost my job and have to tell my family we won't have money coming in…
If the cashier looks at me like I'm stupid when I ask a question…
If I do not have kids and my friend is telling me all about her amazing life as a mom…
If my dad is an alcoholic and my girlfriend sees him drinking …

If I have been divorced and my date asks me about past relationships…
I don't know any statistics about the sports game on tv and my buddies ask me what I thought about last night's game …
I do not have enough money to pay at the counter and other customers are waiting…
I believe in God and my coworker starts to talk about how a pastor made him feel horrible about himself …

What triggers your pain?
What events, what experiences, what moments make you feel horrible about yourself?
When do you feel less as a human?

[*IF* TRIGGER HAPPENS,
THEN I EXPERIENCE PAIN .]

What are your triggers? You have them. **Triggers are everywhere.** Without full awareness of your triggers, it is easy to let these circumstances define you.

High school students often have the same trigger. When someone asks them,
"Where are you going to college?"

College students often have the same trigger. When someone asks them,
"What is your major?"

Recent college graduates often have the same trigger. When someone asks them,
"What are you doing for work?"

You will know your triggers by the pain they cause you, or rather by the pain they trigger in you. Triggers aren't universal. They are yours to own. Triggers hit you uniquely. The things that trigger you will be different than the things that trigger your best friend.

If you haven't yet, ask yourself: what are my triggers?
(Begin to think about this; you don't need a concrete answer yet.)

If _____ happens, then I feel bad about who I am.
Start here. Begin by pinpointing your triggers.

When do you get that feeling like you've been hit by something painful in your gut?

Don't make the mistake of staying surface.
Triggers are easy to confuse. Take advantage of the opportunity and get to the root. What is the real trigger?

You may think someone's peppiness annoys you when really you are just jealous of their accomplishments. You may think someone being late to pick you up annoys you, when really you are triggered by the idea of walking in to work late and having your coworkers give you weird looks. You may think the guy on the plane laughing hysterically is annoying, when really you are annoyed that you haven't gotten any work done the entire flight.
Take the time to look at your triggers in depth. **Pinpoint exactly *which* experience led you to feel pain.**

THE REAL TRIGGER.

Look at the last event that frustrated you. What is the trigger that caused you the pain?

Example: Think about the last time you got frustrated at work. What is the exact reason you felt pain?
Were you triggered *because you made a mistake?*
Were you triggered *because your boss raised his voice at you?*
Were you triggered *because your coworkers laughed at you?*

There is a specific cause or event that led you to the pain you feel.

What triggers you?
If/when _____ happens, then I feel bad internally.
Maybe you're triggered when someone asks, *"Hey, what are you doing with your life?"*…
Maybe you're triggered when reading about someone's extraordinary trip on Facebook…

START LISTING YOUR TRIGGERS

When you go through this next section, take note of any triggers that come to mind so that you don't forget them.

You don't have to know why you are triggered yet, you just have to know what triggers you.

Look for triggers at home, at work, in your relationships, and even in the strangest places. Don't allow yourself to discredit any of your triggers. Most of your triggers will connect to purpose. In fact, almost everything is relevant when it comes to purpose. As noted earlier in the book, I have done life coaching on and off over the last five years. In life coaching, people nearly beg for me to tell them their purpose. The funny thing is when I start by asking about family or work or something that causes them pain, I can see the wheels turning inside of most clients, almost as to say, "Is this relevant to finding my thing?" Certain questions may seem to be irrelevant, but trust the process. Become as aware as you can be of your triggers so that you can understand your pain on a deeper level in order to find what matters most to you.

Remember — your natural instinct may be to problem solve *why* you are feeling pain, or even to start to overcome the pain. The most important thing now is to get all of your triggers out on the table.

What are your triggers? (What are the situations and circumstances that cause you pain?) When you can clarify the painful situations in your life, you'll take the first step toward the root of the problem, and another step toward uncovering your thing.

Good news: Triggers are everywhere. They are easy to find if you know how to find them. I've identified five common places you can find your triggers so that you can see where you are uniquely triggered. Be on the lookout for at least one trigger in each of the five areas, and if you haven't already, start your list of triggers! (Really, start a list of your triggers. You'll need it later to expedite your growth!)

I CAN'T.

A trigger that comes from your inability to do something.
Ex. If I can't get to the gym in the morning, then I feel pain.

You may be frustrated that you can't easily wake up early in the morning. You may be frustrated that you can't go three hours without eating a cookie. You may be frustrated that you can't get a certain girl to pay attention to you. These are examples of *I can't* triggers.

If you can't dance…
If you can't get yourself home on time to see your kids before bed…
Then you feel bad about yourself.
When your inability to do something results in feeling bad about yourself, you are experiencing an Unwritten Rule that stems from the trigger: "I can't."

When do you get frustrated with yourself that you can't do something?

There are probably many things you can't do. I would imagine you can't unicycle and juggle. Does that frustrate you?
Or maybe you can unicycle and juggle, but you can't run a mile in under six minutes. Does that frustrate you?
While there will be many things you can't do, a trigger is only something that affects the way you feel internally.
If you don't care about being skilled at hockey, then it's not a trigger if you can't play hockey.
However, if you see people playing hockey, and you start to experience pain as you remember how horrible you are at the sport, then this is a trigger.

If other people's abilities intimidate you ...
you may have an I can't trigger.

When you look at someone else's ability, is it a reminder of your own lack of ability? If you see or hear about the accomplishments of someone similar to you, is it painful?

If my friend can _____ but I can't…
If my coworker can _____ but I can't….
If my spouse can _____ but I can't…

If my brother can _____ but I can't...

If you were the kid that couldn't take no for an answer ...
you may have an "I can't" trigger.

While it may seem like a positive trait to be the kid that never took no for an answer, you probably have some "I can't" triggers. There are circumstances where you feel less because you don't possess a certain quality or are lacking the same opportunity as someone else.

> *Note: There is a difference between being motivated when you run into something you can't do and letting your worth be destroyed when you can't do something. Know this line: Pursue everything you set your mind to, just be careful about putting your worth into the things you can or can't do. When your worth is in what you can or can't do, your world can come crashing down at any time. Build your worth on a rock, rather than sinking sand, otherwise don't be surprised when you experience painful "I can't "triggers on the daily.*

If you avoid things you are not good at ...
you may have an "I can't" trigger.

You cannot stand to play volleyball because you know you will feel terrible if you lose; so much so that you'd rather not even play volleyball.
(This is also known as a sore loser, and most likely a sore winner.) I hope that you are competitive because it's a great quality to possess. Just be careful about what you are choosing to define your worth and value.

If I can't _____ then I feel pain.
What's the biggest "If I can't _____" that brings you pain?

WHAT IS AN EXAMPLE OF AN "I CAN'T" TRIGGER IN YOUR LIFE?

I DON'T .

The absence of something.

Example: If I don't <u>have the right shoes</u>, then I feel <u>pain</u>.

This trigger comes when you are capable of doing something but you have missed the opportunity or have made the decision not to do it.

I DON'T is about the pain you want to avoid.
You know you will become disappointed, upset, or discouraged with yourself when you don't _____ .

    If I don't get to work early ...
    If I don't finish what I told my boss I would finish ...
    If I don't go out with my friends this weekend ... .
    If I don't _____ then I feel bad about myself.

WHAT IS AN EXAMPLE OF AN "I DON'T" TRIGGER IN YOUR LIFE?

TOO MUCH OR NOT ENOUGH.

Doing something in excess or not doing enough of something.
Example: If I <u>watch Netflix</u> too much, then I feel <u>pain</u>.

If you _____ too much.

    Do you talk too much?
    Do you go out drinking too much?
    Do you sleep in too much?

If you don't _____ enough.

    If you don't workout enough...
    If you don't call her enough...
    If you don't visit them enough ...

Triggers like too much, or not enough, often root from comparison. This is usually a comparison of where others are at or even where they are perceived to be. How much is too much? How much is not enough?

One easy way to find this trigger is to analyze:

Compared to others, I feel bad about who I am because I have more ____ .

Compared to others, I feel bad about who I am because I have less ____ .

WHAT IS AN EXAMPLE OF A "TOO MUCH" OR "NOT ENOUGH" TRIGGER IN YOUR LIFE?

ONLY.

Perceiving yourself to be lacking in a certain area. You are not where others are at, or where you know you could be.

Example: If I only <u>make minimum wage</u>, then I feel <u>pain</u>.

If I only _____ then I feel bad.

If I only got one award at the event…

If I only wrote one book…

If I only watched Netflix today…

How would you fill in that blank?

If I only _____ .

> *Note: Triggers aren't the justification to strive for less. The beauty of growth comes when you no longer feel as though you are less. Or rather, when you do feel less, the most important piece to note is why you feel less. Pinpoint the areas or responses that make you feel like you are less.*

"Only" is often a comparison to a greater idea of who you could or should be.

If I am only the stay at home parent…

If I am only the executive assistant…

If I am only the new employee …

You feel like a let down because you see yourself as only _____ .

WHAT IS AN EXAMPLE OF AN "ONLY" TRIGGER IN YOUR LIFE?

YET.

A rule that indicates you are behind in some way.
Example: If I only make minimum wage, then I feel pain.

If I haven't bought a house yet.
If I haven't lost any weight yet.
If I haven't started my own business yet.
If I haven't _____ yet.

What do you feel "less for" for not having done yet?
With some things, you couldn't care less about being "behind;" those are
not triggers.
While one person is triggered by the idea of not having money saved up for
their children's college fund yet, another is triggered by saving too much and not
enjoying his day-to-day moments.

WHAT IS AN EXAMPLE OF A "YET" TRIGGER IN YOUR LIFE?

BONUS

Find the triggers of yourself and others so that you can change your
relationships. This book won't explain much on relationship dynamics,
but understanding the triggers of others will also be a game changer in
your relationships.

You know you have a "yet" trigger when someone asks you the question "When are you going to…?" and you feel pain.

When are you going to come visit?

When are you going to take the trash out?

When are you going to ask for a raise?

This phrase doesn't even have to be outright said, but the *when* can be implied:

"Are you guys having kids yet?"

"Are you getting married?"

"Is retirement around the corner?"

If someone asks you when, it implies that you haven't done something *yet*. This is painful because it dictates that you are falling behind some standard in some way..

What's the biggest "*when*" question that hits you in the stomach?

TRIGGERS ARE A GIFT.

I once heard marriage explained as the ultimate gift — the gift to see all of your insecurities. I'd like to think that understanding your triggers is a similar gift. Although it may be painful at first, it truly is a gift to understand your pain. The quicker you can understand the pain, the quicker you can move beyond it.

DO NOT MOVE ON FROM THIS CHAPTER UNTIL YOU
LIST AT LEAST THREE OF YOUR TRIGGERS.

EVEN IF YOU ONLY GET THIS:

- Have you ever cringed when you see someone parallel park?
  If yes, that's a trigger.

- Triggers are external events that cause you internal pain.

- Triggers can be found anywhere. They are unique to you.

- Become hyper aware of your triggers so that you can stop the pain.

> *Why it matters to Find Your Thing*
  The pain behind the trigger connects to the deepest place inside of
  you. You need triggers to access that place.

IF YOU STOP READING NOW,
YOU'LL MISS THIS:

*Most people chase their triggers like a hamster on a wheel; But even
with all that motion they aren't making any progress.*

*People deceive themselves by thinking they are moving past the pain,
when in reality they are stuck in the same place.*

The pain will continue to resurface until you get to the deeper issue.

*The next chapter is about getting to your deeper fear, so that you no
longer have to spin your hamster wheel.*

CHAPTER 5

THE HOLE IN YOUR HEART.

HAVE YOU EVER GONE TO SLEEP AT NIGHT IN A VERY COLD PLACE, WITHOUT A BLANKET?

Have you ever gone outside for a walk in the pouring rain, without an umbrella?

Have you ever lounged all day in the sun, in your nice fair skin, without applying sunscreen?

These can be painful experiences.

After a camping experience myself with only one blanket in 40 degree weather, I know how painful it is to sleep without a blanket in a cold place.

Walking in pouring rain can also be a horrible experience. You can quickly go from a few drops ruining your hair to your entire body feeling miserable.

Although I've never been sunburned badly, I've seen the look of terror on people when it hurts to walk and they have to apply aloe vera around the clock.

Pain is rarely fun.

The question is, why did you experience pain?

Did the cold weather freeze you that night, or did you not come prepared with enough blankets?

Did the rain ruin your day, or did you forget to bring the umbrella?

Did you blister up because of the sun, or did you choose not to use sunscreen?

At first, it's not easy to believe, but:

You are often the reason you experience pain.
(Yep. I said it because it's true.) It's easy to blame things outside of your control like the weather, while avoiding personal responsibility in the situation.

Besides the weather, people are one of the easiest external factors to blame for your pain. After all, people wrong you. Strangers aren't the only inconsiderate ones, but often friends, family, and coworkers, too.

What is the one thing that connects your pain from the cold, the rain, and the sun?

What is the one thing that connects your pain from your friends, your family, and your coworkers?

You.
In every situation you are the common denominator. Therefore, you are ultimately some piece of the problem.

You play a role in every problem.
I know it's painful, but it's true.

Think of it like this. You are walking down the street with a group of people and someone makes a comment, but you are the only one that gets offended. Sure, someone else may be in the wrong, but there is a reason why you are getting hurt in that moment.
You are getting hurt, the question is why?

> Rae: "She is so rude. She never says hi to me."
>
> Me: *Why does that cause you pain?*
>
> Rae: "She is not a good friend. I do everything for her."
>
> Me: *No, you're making this about her. I asked you why you are getting hurt. What emotions does it make you feel when she is not excited to see you?*
>
> Rae: "I feel unwanted."

Trigger: Your friend doesn't say hi to you
Deeper Issue: Feeling Unwanted
Unwritten Rule: If she doesn't greet you, then you are unwanted.

The life changing event is not knowing that you are the problem, but understanding why you are the problem. Regardless of what someone said, did, or meant, the question is, why are YOU getting hurt?

Chris: "He didn't listen to what I had to say."

Me: *Why does it bother you that he doesn't listen?*

Chris: "He never listens."

Me: *But why does it bother you? What emotions does it make you feel when he doesn't listen?*

Chris: "Disregarded. I hate feeling disregarded."

Trigger: Someone close to you appears to not be listening.

Deeper Fear: Being disregarded.

Unwritten Rule: If he doesn't listen, then you are disregarded.

Triggers are painful. Yet, triggers are only the surface level of the pain. The reason they sting is due to something much deeper within you. You must shift from focusing on the trigger to focusing on you.

If you understand why you are getting hurt, you will be at a higher level of awareness. At this level of awareness, everything can change.

Brian: "I hate my job. I'm so annoyed at my coworkers."

Me: *Why are you annoyed at your coworkers?*

Brian: "They didn't listen to any of my suggestions today."

Me: *What about that is frustrating?*

Brian: "They never take my suggestions seriously and they looked at me like I was an idiot today. I know what I'm talking about."

Me: *What characteristic does that make you feel?*

Brian: "Like I'm wrong, or incapable. It's the worst feeling ever."

Trigger: Coworkers not listening to your suggestions

Deeper Fear: Feeling incapable.

Unwritten Rule: If your coworkers don't take your suggestions, then you are wrong.

There is always a deeper issue behind pain. Even if you think you're not the problem, you are the problem. The question is why.

Why did the experience cause you pain? What is your deepest fear? Knowing the depths of your fear is invaluable. The depths of your fears help you understand purpose so that you can live a more fulfilling life. Examine the depths behind your trigger.

Unwritten Rule = Trigger + Deeper Fear

The trigger is only the first part of the rule.

[*IF* TRIGGER ,

THEN DEEPER FEAR .]

I hate traffic.

Traffic is one of my triggers, as it probably is for many others. Have you ever driven a longer route just to avoid sitting in traffic? If you're like me, you would do anything to avoid the feeling of sitting in traffic. Weaving in and out of side streets isn't always logical, but it can feel more productive. You may keep moving just to avoid feeling unproductive. Why? On a deeper level, it is likely you want to avoid being an unproductive person. There are certain characteristics you would do anything to avoid. When you find what you are avoiding, you will find the piece you fear.

Traffic is the trigger. It's not the deeper issue. I would do anything to avoid the identity of being an unproductive person.

Being an unproductive person is the deeper fear.

SERIOUSLY, YOU MUST FIND THE ROOT.

I sat down for an introductory life coaching session. The first question I asked Matt was, what are you frustrated with?

"I'm 24. I want to move out of my parents' house."

After further conversation, it turned out that Matt hated living at home — he felt like he was losing his independence by being there.

If I live at home, then I'm not independent.

I could have said, "Alright Matt. I am going to help you. Let's go find a way to get you more income and get out of living in your parent's house."

Instead, I went for the root of the problem. It turns out it wasn't necessarily moving out or even the lack of independence that was the root of Matt's pain. Matt was feeling horrible about himself because he didn't feel respectable. Not just at home but at work and anywhere in life for that matter. Matt went on to tell me more about how his role at work was also frustrating because he didn't feel like the other guys respected him.

Do you see how it is easy to miss the deeper fear (the root) with something more surface?

Step One: Identify the Trigger

Matt's trigger - living at home

If you focus only on the trigger, like moving out of your parent's house, you will often miss the fear, like the need for independence.

Step Two: Identify the Fear

Matt's fear - not being independent

If you only focus on the immediate fear that comes to mind, like not being independent, you will often miss the deeper fear.

Step Three: Write Down Your Unwritten Rule

Matt's rule - If I live at home, then I'm not independent

Step Four: Find Your Deeper Fear

Matt's deeper fear - not being respectable

If I am (fear) then I am (deeper fear).

Step Five: Find the Root (Optional)

Matt's deepest fear - that he doesn't belong.

Often, there will be an even deeper fear.

Repeat until you find the deepest fear — the root.

If I am (deeper fear) then I am (deepest fear).

Root:

Your deepest fear.

THE ROOT.

What is your root? Your root is your deepest fear. This is the place that it hurts.

While moving out of his parents' house might have delayed some of Matt's pain, it would eventually come back because Matt didn't address the deeper issue behind the trigger. Without looking beneath the trigger, you miss the real fear and eventually the real value.

Many of us share common deep rooted fears. While you and I may be triggered in different ways, it is likely that most of your pain is rooted in the same few issues.

Here is the truth. You are the problem. (Okay, you're not the entire problem, but you play a significant role.) The great thing about this is that you can change the pain. Since you are part of the cause of pain, you are also part of the solution. The power to change your circumstances comes from knowing your root. Your root is the source of your pain.

WHAT IS THE ROOT OF YOUR PAIN?

Now you are going to do a 5-step activity to find your deeper fear. (Do not skip this.)

Take five focused minutes. This is the most important piece of the entire book to *Find Your Thing*.

This is not something you can breeze through easily, and I encourage you to be thoughtful and take as long as you need. Put it down and come back to it if you need to. Eventually this will become an automatic process for your mind.

I must warn you, you've done things that have been more fun than this exercise. There may be about 280 things that you'd rather do, but I encourage you to push through because what's on the other end is pure gold.

DO NOT SKIP ANY PART OF THE NEXT SECTION.

FOLLOW THIS TEMPLATE.
(Use the previous two pages if needed for reference.)

STEP 1: IDENTIFY A TRIGGER.

What is one recent moment that caused you internal pain and discomfort?

STEP 2: IDENTIFY THE ROOT.

What does this moment show you that you fear?

STEP 3: WRITE DOWN YOUR UNWRITTEN RULE.

Write it out using the two responses above.
If _____ then I am _____.
　　(TRIGGER)　　　　　　　　　(FEAR)

STEP 4: FIND YOUR DEEPER FEAR.

Identify the deeper fear behind your fear.
If I am _____ then I am _____.
　　　(FEAR)　　　　　　　　(DEEPER FEAR)

STEP 5: REPEAT THIS STEP TO FIND YOUR DEEPEST FEAR/ROOT
ISSUE (DEEPEST FEAR = ROOT ISSUE)

If I am _____ then I am _____.
　　(DEEPER FEAR)　　　　　　(DEEPEST FEAR)

LITMUS TEST

List three recent triggers in other areas of life that also lead you to that same deeper fear.

If _____ then I am MY DEEPEST FEAR.

Trigger #1:

Trigger #2:

Trigger #3:

Note: Most of your triggers come back to the same root. If you can see three other recent triggers that are rooted in the same fear, then you are probably spot on, or at least pretty close to identifying your deepest fear. If it doesn't resonate with you, start back at the beginning with a different trigger.

WHAT IS YOUR IDENTITY ISSUE?

Use the template on the last page, or walk through it by going through your triggers and your fears.

TRIGGERS (WHAT CAUSED YOU PAIN).

Bring your triggers to the surface so that you can look to your deeper fears.

Note: I do this daily. I am constantly reflecting on my triggers. Collect your triggers.

What triggers have you noticed from the last chapter that bring you pain?

What triggers have you noticed this week alone, at work, at home, or with your friends?

What are the ongoing triggers you can't seem to shake; they just keep appearing time after time?

THE ROOT (WHY DOES YOUR TRIGGER CAUSE YOU PAIN?)

Look behind the trigger to examine the deeper reason for your pain.

What is your deepest fear? Based on your triggers, what are the characteristics that you work to avoid feeling and becoming?

You must dive into why. Why are these triggers causing you pain? What is the deeper identity question you are looking to fill?

Look at your fears and answer:

What is your deepest fear?

Based on your triggers, what are the characteristics that you work to avoid feeling and becoming?

Incompetent

Alone

Unwanted

A failure

Not accepted

Forgotten

A bad person

Not good enough

Dependent

If you are distraught because someone won't forgive you (trigger) ...

Do you fear being unwanted (root issue)?

If you feel insecure because someone doesn't respect you (trigger) ...
Do you fear being forgotten (root issue)?

If you can't stand that your love isn't being reciprocated (trigger) ...
Do you fear being incompetent (root issue)?

You will notice many of the same root fears will continue to appear. Your fears are deeply rooted. Triggers lead to pain because you fear becoming certain characteristics.
What characteristics are you trying to avoid? Identify the root of your triggers.

Trigger: Your friend offers you a piece of cake. All of a sudden, you think about gaining weight and it causes you internal pain.

Root: The question is why? If the thought of gaining five pounds disturbs you, what is the deeper fear? If I gain another five pounds, then I am _____.
    ...a failure?
    ...incompetent?
    ...alone?
    ...unwanted?
    ...forgotten?
    ...unaccepted?
    ...not good enough?
    ...a bad person?
    ...dependent?

Trigger: You see a couple holding hands on the sidewalk. All of a sudden you think about getting married and it causes you internal pain.

Root: The question is why? If the thought of marriage disturbs you, what is the deeper fear? If I don't get married by age 30, then I am _____.
    ...a failure?
    ...incompetent?
    ...alone?
    ...unwanted?
    ...forgotten?

…unaccepted?

…not good enough?

…a bad person?

…dependent?

IT'S ALL ABOUT IDENTITY.

Your root is your deepest fear. You know how sometimes it feels painful when you are trying to figure out who you are? When you are trying to find your voice?

Identity is knowing who you are.
Your deeper fear — your root — is the hole in your identity that you are missing.

Triggers and rules trace back to your search for identity.

Oh…you didn't realize that your search for purpose is actually a search for identity? I know. I couldn't tell you that earlier. I couldn't lead with, "read this book to figure out your identity" because that's scary. No one wants to talk about identity. Knowing where you lack identity is key to seeing your purpose. Knowing how you lack identity is key to knowing and understanding who you are and what you care about on this earth.

Lack of purpose is a lack of identity.

Purpose exists in identity.

Everything ultimately roots back to your question of identity. You can ignore it, but it doesn't get you anywhere. I ignored the concept of identity for multiple years, because I didn't like the word identity. It seemed fluffy, even though identity is the strength of who you are.

Identity is where you put your stake in the ground to declare who you are. Identity is nothing to run from but everything to run toward.

What's my thing? is a cry for "**What's my identity?**"

The question of, "Who am I?"

You are starting to see your triggers. Now you must look deeper to see the true pain point, the true core of your problem — your identity issue.

Identity is not a new concept. People everywhere speak about identity because it's a real thing. In fact, identity is a cornerstone of life. Jon Stewart, one of the brilliant minds that influenced me as I studied to become a life coach, explains that there are three pieces of identity most people seek. People everywhere are searching to answer three questions about themselves:

1. Am I competent?
2. Am I a good person?
3. Am I worthy of love?

When you are in conflict with other people, Stewart explains that the issue roots back to one of these three identity questions. I am not saying these three are each triggers. In the search for purpose, especially when you are surrounded by other people who have already found what they are good at, how do these three questions come up for you?

"Am I competent?"
Do I have something great in me?
Do I have a unique purpose?

"Am I a good person?"
Other people seem to care about something…do I care about anything?
A good person invests their time in something that matters…does anything even matter to me?

"Am I worthy of love?"
If I haven't found my purpose, am I defective in some way?
Is some part of me missing?

Am I this?
Am I that?
Am I …?
Am I …?
Am I …?
Who am I?

When your identity is in constant question, it is difficult to see purpose.
When your identity is in constant question, it is difficult to live a life
of fulfillment.
When your identity is in constant question, it is difficult to live a life for the

things you value.

Lack of identity sucks.

The only thing that sucks more than lacking identity is not being aware of your own identity issues.

Choosing to avoid or ignoring your identity question does not mean you don't lack it. You are human, you have an identity issue. Embrace it and continue to increase your awareness, or don't expect to grow from it.

DO NOT MOVE ON FROM THIS CHAPTER UNTIL YOU —
IDENTIFY YOUR DEEPEST FEAR.

EVEN IF YOU ONLY GET THIS:

- Your pain is not about the trigger. Behind every trigger is a deeper pain point.

- You must look at the reason you are getting hurt from the trigger? • Every person has a deeper fear. (Go back and read this chapter if you haven't landed on your deeper fear.

- Your deeper fear is also referred to as your identity issue (the hole in your identity).

- Most of your triggers will root back to the same identity issue.

> *Why it matters to Find Your Thing*
  Your deepest fear is connected to your deepest value. From your deepest value stems purpose and your thing.

TRIGGER > DEEPER FEAR > DEEPEST FEAR

43

IF YOU STOP READING NOW,
YOU'LL MISS THIS:

My team and I spent over a year organizing a weekend leadership event for over 1,200 students. It was a grueling year that tested all of us. The last night of the event, I was standing in front of my team explaining to them how proud I was of all of the hard work they had done. While I was speaking to them I started bawling. I remember trying to stop myself, but the emotion was just too powerful. I was proud of them and proud of myself. I was inspired by them and inspired by myself. In the midst of both pain and purpose, I cried.

People cry. Sometimes when they're happy, sometimes when they're hurt.
People don't realize that pain and purpose are rooted in the same place.

Think about the last time you cried tears of joy; a powerful emotion came over you and the only response that made sense was to cry.

For example, a mother crying when she holds her newborn child for the first time or a man crying as his bride walks down the aisle. These people are experiencing deep emotion through tears.

Alternatively, a mother losing her child or a man experiencing the heartbreak of divorce from his bride are also experiencing deep emotion through tears.

In both situations, the child is important to the mother and the bride is important to the man. Happiness and sadness are sourced from the same place.

Most people try to keep pain and purpose separate. They approach the two as an "either/or" situation. "Once I find my purpose, I'll get rid of my pain." The presence of one does not mean the absence of the other.

Most people stop dead in their tracks at the sight of pain. Pain is proof that something matters to you. On the other end of pain you will always find purpose.

CHAPTER 6

WHAT DO I DO WITH THIS PAIN?

I'VE LANDED ON MY DEEPER FEAR, NOW WHAT?

You did it.

You've found the hole. You got to the awareness of your deepest fear —
your root.

If you choose, you no longer have to run around like a crazy person, fighting
the surface level problems that are only bringing you back to the same pain over
and over again. You no longer have to spend time and energy solving the wrong
problem because you've found what's really going on at the deeper level.

By understanding your deepest level of pain, you no longer have to live in what
you have been doing. You have created two new opportunities that most people
never find access to, including the opportunity to *Find Your Thing*.

If there are three doors, three choices, you previously only had access to Door #1.

Self awareness is the difference. Your new found awareness is what gives you two
more options.

DOOR #1: YOUR DEFAULT OPTION

*What most people do with pain because it's easier or because they haven't unlocked
other options.*

Most people live in door number one — the default option of getting rid of this pain as quickly as possible, often by looking externally to fill the need. (I call this a massive unproductive effort that results in destruction.)

Most people look externally to fill the need of their pain. **Looking externally for internal answers robs of you of your joy.** The answer you seek is not external.

When you look externally, you rely on the world for validation. This is dangerous for you and dangerous for others. **You walk around in life empty and put your insecurity on others.**

Tell me I'm important!
Tell me I'm respectable!
Tell me I'm valued!
Tell me I'm desirable!
Tell me I'm capable!

When the people around you don't validate you in the ways you need, you are left frustrated. You are unhappy with other people, and then carry internal dissatisfaction. **You lose a bit of yourself and you create destruction in the lives of those around you.**

This approach to living with pain is not sustainable. Dealing with triggers and your deepest fears externally is like going through your spam emails. When you go through and delete them one by one it's frustrating. You spend time and energy deleting them only to sign in the next day and find there are more. They haven't left you. They keep coming back.

Pursuing external solutions every time you are in pain is not sustainable. The pain will continue to surface. **If you want to *Find Your Thing*, before you get caught up in short term external solutions, you have to know that the secret sauce to purpose is internal.**

Luckily, your awareness has unlocked two other options.

MAGIC DOOR #2: (GROWTH)
Learning how to work through your pain so that it doesn't bring destruction to yourself and those around you.

When you say, "I want a thing" and "I want to know my purpose," the majority of the time it's not purpose you seek. Usually the tugging on your heart that you feel, the longing that won't leave you, is actually a longing to fill this hole in your identity.

When people say, *"I want to know my purpose because I want to help people,"* they are usually saying, *"I want something in my life that completes me. I am incomplete and looking for something to fill the hole inside of me."*

Did you catch that? **People often mistake their need for purpose with their identity issue.** When you hear people talk about finding their thing, they are really talking about the painful hole in their identity.

Keeping this hole wide open will inhibit you from being the person you desire to be.

Now that you know the truth behind your pain, you can work through it. To work through your pain means to minimize the damage by making your insecurity smaller. When you decrease the size of your identity issue, you will relieve yourself of a massive amount of pain.

Instead of filling your need externally, if you look internally you can close the gap. You are holding on to many things that are keeping this hole open. **Now you can look inside to see how you can repair that hole so that you no longer have to live less of the life you were called to live.**

The second section of this book will take you through door #2.

MAGIC DOOR #3 (PURPOSE):
Learning how to shift focus from your fears to your purpose so that you can live a life of greatness. (You know how you've been wanting the magic door to purpose to open up. Well, here it is.)

Many people are frustrated that they are not living or pursuing their thing, when the reality is – how could they be while they are living in fear? How can you expect to live out your thing when you are only focused on fear?

What you focus on becomes your reality. If you focus on the fear, that's that's all you will ever see.

Living in purpose will not come from focusing on your fear. Purpose doesn't come from fear, it comes from value. To live out of fear is to run from something. **To live out of value means to run *for* something.**

To live out of fear means to have an absence of something. **To live out of value means to have an overflow of something.**

There is a distinct difference.

The good news is now that you understand your deeper fear, you have created the opportunity to see your deeper value.

Pain and purpose are rooted in the same place. People often run from the things that cause pain, and yet, pain is directly connected to a place of purpose. There are a million ways to find what really matters, but pain is one of the fastest. Your pain cuts to what matters most at the core of your heart and at the core of your identity.

To *Find Your Thing*, all you have to do is make one simple shift from focusing on your fear to your value.

The third section of this book will take you through door #3.

EVEN IF YOU ONLY GET THIS:

- Most people never experience purpose because they live their entire life focusing on the pain. They run around desperately seeking for others to solve their insecurities, including their deepest fear. (I call this Door #1: The Default Option.)

- Growth allows you to work through your pain so that it doesn't cause as much damage to yourself and others. (I call this Door #2: Growth.)

- Pain and purpose can coexist. It's not an either/or. You do not have to have one or the other. In fact, your pain is one of the biggest opportunities for purpose. (I call this Door #3: Purpose. You can read more about this in section 3)

IF YOU STOP READING NOW,
YOU'LL MISS THIS:

Section Two: GROWTH.

Make the shift from pain to growth.

No longer do you have to drown in your pain. To get to a place of sustainable fulfillment, to become everything you are destined for, you must choose growth. Section 2 is about growth – how to move beyond your pain to true satisfaction. With less fear in your life, you can live a more sustainable life of freedom.

Section Three: PURPOSE.

Make the shift from pain to purpose.

No longer do you have to be afraid of your identity issue. Section three is about how to clarify your purpose so that you can operate for a greater mission. As you walk around day to day, are you stressed by your pain, or have you decided to use it as an opportunity for purpose? Purpose exists; it's just been hidden in the pain. Section 3 is about pursuing the greatest value in your life and officially Find Your Thing.

SECTION 2

GROWTH.

CHAPTER 7

MOVE BEYOND YOUR PAIN.

I HAVE A FEAR OF BEING COLD.

If I'm cold, I can't focus. I can't read. I can't write. I can barely hear myself think. Until I move beyond my pain, I can't bring myself to focus on anything else. (If you've ever been to or lived in Michigan, you may share this same fear.)

Maybe you have a fear of upsetting your boss. You can't even begin working on a project until you know it is exactly what she asked you to do.

Maybe you have a fear of disappointing your mother-in-law. You won't be able to enjoy yourself unless the house is clean for her when she comes over.

When you are constantly being hit and your identity is questioned, it's painful.
It's hard to see anything beyond fear when fear is present.
What most people do when they have pain:
"God, please tell me my purpose. I don't want to feel this way anymore!"

People often grow so unsatisfied in pain that they beg for God to change their circumstances.

Consider this: Instead of begging God for things to change, what if YOU changed? What if you changed so that you could not only handle the things around you, but create the change you have been waiting for?

[*IF* YOU WORK THROUGH YOUR PAIN, *THEN* YOU'LL HAVE A GREATER CAPACITY FOR PURPOSE.]

This is growth.

Most people would rather sit in the pain, waiting for someone or something to rescue them and fill their hole.

"God please come in and magically fill this hole in my heart, then I'll be fulfilled. Oh, and if it's cool with you God, I want to stay exactly the same. I want things around me to change, but I don't want to change."

Even though God is able to make magic happen, a magical move on His part will not solve your problems. Even if God moved you into new circumstances, you will still be the same person. To take on bigger challenges, you must become the person that can lead others in a bigger way. You must grow. Purpose is not about circumstances changing ... it's about you changing. It's growth.

Martin Luther King did big work because of who he was, not because something magically changed in his life. He could have sat suffering, frustrated and hoping that something would change. Instead, he changed. He took action.

To move beyond your pain doesn't mean you have to solve it, but it does mean you have to understand your pain and begin to work through it. Learning how to work through your pain is what gives you the muscle to take on bigger challenges.

Change yourself and then you change the world.

I know you are dying for purpose. The great thing is that when you work through your rules, you develop an ability to see greater purpose.
It's easy to stay in the pain or try a quick fix rather than addressing the root issues.

3 REASONS YOU MIGHT NEVER ESCAPE THE PAIN:

1. YOU IGNORE THE PAIN.

Ignoring the pain may seem like a solution, but oftentimes it only gets worse. The problem is, most people don't even realize the depths at which they are ignoring their pain.

2. YOU RUN FROM PAIN.

You avoid something by looking to escape as quickly as possible.

I am not happy with this job. I need to leave.

I am not happy with this relationship. I need to leave.

I am not happy with this house. I need to leave.

Are you frustrated at work, wanting to leave because you are questioning, "Am I good enough?" While most people want to leave the job so they can leave the pain, the truth is, if you walk around with the identity gap of — Am I good enough? — you will bring that with you wherever you go. You'll bring that to every job and to every relationship and to every attempt of living out your purpose. You may move jobs or relationships, but the root issue will always be present. To alleviate suffering, the real issues must be addressed.

People not only run away, but run toward something else that is actually a cheaper version of what they really desire.

I can't tell you how many times I have heard clients say "Lisa…THIS is what I need. A job like this." They have quickly convinced themselves that one new thing will solve all of their problems. Most of us do this. This even happens to insightful people — one of my friends, in fact. He uttered those same words to me. "Lisa…THIS is what I need. A job like this." Three months later, he came back and said, "You were right. The new job wasn't the answer." I knew a quick fix — changing jobs — wouldn't solve his pain, but it looks like he had to find that out for himself.

THE DANGER IS THAT YOU NEVER FILL YOUR HOLE.

What most people don't realize is that the hole in identity doesn't magically disappear. In fact, it's quite the opposite. Identity gaps will stay with you wherever you go.

3. YOU GIVE UP.

People often grow so defeated from fighting the pain that they give up when they don't think they have control. The pain is so overwhelming that giving up seems easier than trying to work through it.

This doesn't have to be a conscious waving of the white flag. Some people don't even realize they've already given up. They are no longer battling to work through the pain because they don't know how to get to purpose.

While ignoring pain, running from it, or giving up seem to be solutions, the truth is that none of these solve the root problem of pain. Section two is growing from the root of the pain.

EVEN IF YOU ONLY GET THIS:

- Your purpose will expand or deflate based on your growth. When it comes to pain, it's easier to:

  1. Ignore the pain.
  2. Run from pain.
  3. Give up.

- Pain is inevitable, so the best response to pain is growth.

  If you want purpose, growth is the single thing that expands your purpose.

IF YOU STOP READING NOW,
YOU'LL MISS THIS:

Before you swing, you better know what you are aiming for. Trying to grow from your pain can look an awful lot like swinging a bat at a pinata after spinning around five times in a circle blindfolded.

Trying to work through your identity issue can feel an awful lot like playing Super Smash Brothers for the first time, pushing random buttons because you have no idea which button is to jump, which is to shield, and which is to roundhouse kick your opponent in the face. (Oh, that wasn't you? Well, I never knew what I was doing in video games.)

It doesn't have to be so difficult, you just have to be willing to work through it.

There are five ways to grow beyond your pain and into purpose.

5 Ways to Move Through Your Pain:

1. Get to the Root.
   (Find your deepest fear.)
2. Expose the Origin.
   (Where did this rule come from?)
3. Challenge the Truth.
   (Is it true?)
4. Cut off the lie.
   (Separate yourself from the rule.)

ADVANCED:

5. Rewrite Your Story.
   (Change the meaning.)

The more you invest in these next five chapters will directly affect the sustainability of your fulfilment and how you live out your purpose.

CHAPTER 8

GET TO THE ROOT.

MOST PEOPLE ARE CONDITIONED TO RUN FROM PAIN, BECAUSE THEY AREN'T TAUGHT HOW TO WORK THROUGH IT.

After you are aware of your pain, the goal is to move toward the awareness of your deeper fear (your root) — and own it. Until you accept accountability for why you are getting hurt, you will not be able to work through it.

Here is a recap on how to move from pain to ownership of your root (your deeper fear).

> *Note: This process may take a few minutes at first, but eventually you can move through this quickly and almost subconsciously. It becomes as natural to you as driving. It's scary, but you realize you are doing it without even thinking.*

STEP 1: ACKNOWLEDGE YOUR PAIN.

Seems simple enough, right? The next time you are frustrated, annoyed, sad or experiencing any emotional pain, start here.

Make a mental or physical note that you are in pain. This takes less than a second to do, then immediately move to pinpoint your trigger.

STEP 2: IDENTIFY YOUR TRIGGER.

What caused your pain?
Every Unwritten Rule starts with a trigger; the skill is identifying the *actual* trigger.

Say in your head, "I am in pain because ... " or write down your trigger on a notepad, in your phone, etc.

If you incorrectly identify the trigger, you may be headed down the wrong path. Get to the root. What is the actual trigger in your situation?

Even a slight variation of understanding the trigger will throw you off.

QUESTION YOUR TRIGGER.

Ask yourself a few times over to make sure you have the right trigger. At first it will take a few minutes, but after a while, it will become natural.

The more you practice your awareness and reflection, the better and quicker you will get at identifying the trigger.
"Is it A or is it really B that triggered my frustration?"

Go to the moment you were frustrated. Dissect the trigger.
Example: If you are frustrated after work ... is the trigger your boss giving you more work to do OR your coworker laughing?

What is the actual event/experience that brought you internal pain?
Begin to ask yourself what the actual trigger was?
Identify your most recent trigger.

STEP 3: IDENTIFY YOUR ROOT.

Why are you in pain?
Once you know what caused your pain, it's time to see why.

When your coworker gave you that look, it triggered you. You were frustrated. Now the question is why. What about this situation is allowing YOU to be hurt? Bring it back to yourself. Get to the deeper fear. The key in all of this is identifying why you got hurt.

It does you no help to say...
"My coworker was rude. My coworker is the problem."

The quicker you can get to the root of what is paining you, the quicker you can move beyond it.

What about you is getting hurt? What piece of identity are you looking to be validated?

Example: "*When my coworker looked at me that way ... it made me feel stupid. I hate when my intelligence is questioned.*"

Unwritten Rule: If my coworker gives me the look, then I am stupid.
Trigger: Look from my coworker
Root: Intelligence

In the moments when you get triggered, your value is questioned. What identity are you avoiding?

QUESTION YOUR ROOT.
"Is A or is B the real reason I am in pain?"
Go to the pain you felt or are still feeling. Dissect the identity gap.
Example: If you are frustrated after your coworker gave you the look, are you experiencing pain because you feel stupid ... or you feel alone?

Be aware. Be accountable that the problem started with you. Once you can accept that and agree with that truth then you can move on to the next step. If you never accept the rule, then you're trapped and you can't move on. *Most people can't accept that something inside of them is causing the pain - not the external factor.*

If you misidentify a trigger or your identity gap, and you still feel like crap, then you've probably identified the wrong rule. Then ask yourself, is *this* really what is causing me pain or is it something else? If you identify the right trigger, and can get to the real root issue, then you are at least fighting the necessary battle; at least you are climbing the right mountain.

The next time you have discomfort:
  1. Acknowledge your pain.
  2. Identify your trigger.
  3. Identify your root.

These three steps are what it means to own your pain and your root. Ownership is key in emotional intelligence.

BUT WHY ARE YOU IN PAIN?

In day-to-day situations, the ability to ask and answer, *"What is causing me pain and why?"* is life changing. This is emotional intelligence. Identifying the reason you are in pain will not only save you time from blaming and complaining, but lead you to the first step to true growth. Understanding what and why you have pain will allow you to move from your pain. Recognizing the rule at hand – **IF ____ THEN ____** – means you have not only found the trigger, but also the reason behind the pain.

EVEN IF YOU ONLY GET THIS:

- The next time you are in pain, acknowledge it.

[*IF* TRIGGER ,
THEN IDENTITY ISSUE .]

- Identity your trigger. What caused you the pain?

- Identify your root. Why are you in pain?

- Being able to recognize "I've seen this before…this is my search for identity" will save you a lot of time trying to solve the problem of your trigger, and instead spend the time investing in your root issue.

IF YOU STOP READING NOW,
YOU'LL MISS THIS:

Have you ever found something at a garage sale and later realized it was worth a lot more than the $5 you paid for it? What a great feeling.

A woman named Teri Horton went to a thrift store to purchase a gift for a friend of hers. The cashier asked for $8 and Teri bargained until she reluctantly settled for the $5 painting. Teri described the painting as ugly but wanted the gift for her friend. Her friend also thought the picture was ugly so Teri attempted to sell it at her garage sale. When a local art teacher saw the painting, he informed her that it may be a Jackson Pollock. Sure enough, the painting was not only created by Jackson Pollock, but was worth millions. Teri sold the painting for $50 million.

How can something fluctuate so much in value? How does one decide if something is worth $5 or $50 million?

Maybe the reverse has happened to you. Maybe you purchased something at a high price only to realize it wasn't worth a dime.

The truth is, origin is everything. You can value something your entire life without knowing the true origin. Without the true origin the value might be skewed.

The origin matters.

In the next chapter, you'll look at the origin behind your rules. Once you discover the source of your rules, you can decide whether or not your rules have the value of a dollar store painting or a Jackson Pollock.

CHAPTER 9

EXPOSE THE ORIGIN.

WHERE DID IT BEGIN?

Your identity, the person you believe you are, stems from your deepest fears.
Your deepest fears – originated from somewhere. Now the question is, where did
your deeper fear(s) come from?

Many people are influenced by parenting, or honestly, a lack of parenting. It is
easy to grow up in this world wounded with questions like "Am I loved?" "Am I
capable?" "Am I a good person?" that stem from parenting. When you aren't sure
of your identity, you put up rules so that you can try to fill that hole.
If I get other people to laugh, then I am lovable.
If I keep everything in my life tidy, then I am a good girl.
Rules started when you were young – it's important to look at where they
came from.

Honestly, it's not just parenting that creates our rules. **From the moment
you were born, you have been surrounded by influences. These influences,
unconsciously and subconsciously, have shaped your beliefs, your fears, and
therefore, your Unwritten Rules.** Your perception of self originated from
someone or something.

Did you grow up listening to friends that valued hard work or condemned working hard?

Did you grow up learning from teachers that wanted you to succeed or teachers that were out to get you?

Did you grow up around family that told you you'd never amount to anything or family that praised you?

There was an interesting study performed on people sentenced to jail. The study found the one massive factor that indicated whether or not someone would end up in jail. Can you guess the number one factor? It wasn't socio-economic status and it wasn't skin color. The number one factor that determined whether or not someone would end up in jail was whether or not they had friends in jail. There is a clear correlation that the people in jail are those surrounded by others that also ended up in jail. The type of people you are friends with is a lead indicator for who you will become.

> *"You are an average of the 5 people you spend the most time with."*

JIM ROHN

People love this quote. This quote freaks me out. It illustrates how crucial the people that you surround yourself with are. The people around you play a role in shaping your thoughts and decisions. The way those around you perceive value will have an effect on how you perceive value.

What do you get praised for?

What do you get called out for not doing?

If stealing or committing certain crimes is valued by those around you, it increases the likelihood that you will value that as well – hence why your peer group determines whether or not you will be in jail.

YOUR CHOICES HAVE ALREADY BEEN DETERMINED FOR YOU.

There is a default decision making that exists for your choices, based on your influences. **You make decisions without choosing because someone chose for**

you, long before you realized. You often don't see this default because it requires conscious awareness and then conscious effort. Before continuing to live on and accepting the rules that have been created for you, let's expose the root. You found where you lack identity, but where did that rule come from? *Where do these rules come from? Where did your root originate?*

When you look to the root of your rule, it can be tempting to want to blame the source. It's easy to shift the blame of your pain to your horrible parents, your inadequate teachers, or your lazy friends. Blame diffuses the responsibility and means you don't have to be accountable for your actions. However, blaming limits you. If you blame anyone outside of yourself, that means your actions are determined by the decisions of others. That is not entirely true. You have control over your decisions.

I love being able to take responsibility for myself because that also gives me the ability to have control over my thoughts and beliefs. While it is not productive to blame society as whole, it is important to see what has been pre-construed by society. Find the default rule that has existed, then you can decide on your own if you agree or disagree with the truth you have been living from.

THE DEFAULT RULE OF SOCIETY.

You must understand the default that has been placed on your decision making if you ever desire to change it. Before you had the chance to set your own opinion, it had already been determined for you by society. Again, that's scary.

Which has more value?

Good looking or not good looking
20K salary or 200K salary
Clean house or messy house
All C student or all A student
1 like on Instagram or 1000 likes on Instagram
Having a job or being unemployed

People don't realize that they don't create their own rules; rules were first created for them.

You see, society has already created a scale of worth. Whether you agree with the scale or not, it's hard to break free from.

In most cases, society as a whole has already dictated that …

If you are good looking…

If you make more money…

If your house is clean…

Then you are more *worthy*.

Look at each of your rules.

Example: *If I can't keep a relationship, then I am not a good catch.*

Where did this concept come from?

(Was it friends? Family? The media? Was it something someone once said?)

All of these "rules" have been predetermined for you. **Rules are often attributed to an anonymous society, but the truth is you have been directly influenced by your culture, your family, and other people that surround you.**

DIFFERENT GROUPS OF PEOPLE ENCOURAGE DIFFERENT RULES.

What is your family's default?

Maybe your family struggles to make ends meet. What you have been raised to believe will change everything.

If you are working really hard to earn money, then you are strong.

OR

If you are working really hard to earn money, then you are failing.

What is the default for your friend group? What is the default for your coworkers? What is the default for your age group? What is the default for your gender? What is the default for your culture?

I have a Filipino friend that was expected to be a nurse by her family and culture. If you are a nurse, then you are a *better* Filipino woman. Another friend of mine that grew up as a Pakistani-American explained that it was more honorable for him to date a Pakistani woman. If you date a Pakistani woman, then you are a *better* Pakistani man.

If you want to identify the default rules that are present in your life, look at the people in your life. Look at those you grew up with and those that you have allowed to influence you. You don't accept all of the rules around you (if you did, you would never be able to make a decision), but the rules you carry originated from somewhere. Where did they come from?

DIFFERENT RULES COME FROM DIFFERENT STAGES OF LIFE.

I remember when it was time for me to choose a college, I knew it was more valued by my family to go to a prestigious school. Living in the state of Michigan, that meant the University of Michigan was the best option.

If you go to a prestigious school, then you are more important.

What was valued in your high school? Which type of students were valued most?
In my high school, it was thought that students were more valuable:
You had all A's ...
You were a star athlete ...
You were able-bodied, rather than disabled ...
You hung out with the popular crowd ...
High school, like any stage in life, created a scale of worth, leaving many people using this to measure their worth and their success.

I DON'T THINK RULES APPLY TO ME.

You might be thinking, not all students want to have all A's. Not all students want to be the star athlete. Not all students want to hang out with the popular crowd. **Each person is influenced by many factors that contribute to their unique set of rules.** One student might believe he is worth more if he makes a lead role in the play, where another is focused on leading the marching band. Another student might care more about getting rejected upon asking someone to the homecoming dance, when another cares about getting made fun of for asking for extra help from a teacher. Rules vary.
Remember: Your rules are different than the person next to you. While certain things may have been imprinted on us, even if you believe the opposite, the rule

may be prevalent in your life. If you pursue the opposite of what is expected, if you are able to rebel, then you are valuable and courageous.

No one is exempt from rules. They might look different. They might change. But either way there are rules that influence you. You must see the rules so that you can have a better understanding of the expectations that were created in your life. The expectations that you intentionally, or often unintentionally, started to believe.

EXPOSE THE ROOT.

What is the reason you believe the rule:

[*IF* TRIGGER ,

THEN IDENTITY GAP .]

Where did it come from — your desire to feel important?
Where did it come from — your desire to feel like you have it all together?
Where did it come from — your desire to feel helpful?

Society…family…culture…friends…strangers…coworkers…customers… thought leaders…famous athletes…Influence can come from anywhere. The root of the identity question will vary and its impact will vary.

Seeing the origin allows you to see the full truth. It doesn't matter where your rules come from, but what matters is what you do about them once you expose the origin.

EVEN IF YOU ONLY GET THIS:

- Rules exist in your life that you may not even realize.

- The more you can expose the source of your beliefs, the more you can choose for yourself what you desire to believe.

- The next time you experience a trigger and you look to understand your pain, ask yourself where this belief rooted from. (Family? Friends? Culture? Society?

- When you know the source, you can see the full truth.

IF YOU STOP READING NOW,
YOU'LL MISS THIS:

It was the first day of eighth grade science. Mr. Renius pulled out a globe and asked our class what seemed to be a simple question,

"Which way is up?"

Forty-eight minutes later, we found ourselves in the middle of what seemed like a never-ending discussion. Was there a true up? What if the globe was upside down our whole lives? Who was the ultimate authority that got to decide?

Most people live their lives believing certain truths about who they are without ever really questioning them. The next chapter will explore what is true.

CHAPTER 10

CHALLENGE THE TRUTH.

PLATO'S ALLEGORY OF THE CAVE was one of the most influential pieces I read in high school english.

Three prisoners had grown up their entire life in a cave. There is a walkway outside of the cave and a fire burning behind it, so every time someone or something goes through the walkway, the prisoners see a shadow in front of them.

The prisoners have grown up their entire life in the cave and can only see in front of them. As a result, the shadows are the reality for the prisoners. Shadows are what they refer to as people, because it's all they have ever seen. The human voices and laughter match up with a shadow. The shadows are the real thing.

One day, one of the prisoners escapes, only to realize his entire life had been a lie. He came back to tell the other prisoners, but the prisoners believe he is delusional. They believe he was harmed by the outside world and kill him.

The question becomes — what is reality?
Are you seeing the Truth or a modified version of truth?
Just because something has always been true to you would be difficult to know as the ultimate truth.

What are you believing as truth that was never really truth to begin with?

The next few chapters exist to challenge your perception of truth — for you to decide for yourself what is true, which rules you want to believe, and which rules are a lie.

Is it true if *they* say it is true?

Who are *they* anyway, and how can we be sure they know truth?

To challenge the truth means to break everything down so that you can clearly see what exists.

Is it true?

Break it down for yourself. You'll never know unless you poke holes and question everything.

Some things will be true. Some things will be false. Some things will be so close to the truth, that it will become easy to confuse it with the truth. That is why we must break everything down to see for ourselves.

What we believe to be true changes everything. **We must examine our truths to make sure they are accurate. While truth doesn't change, your perception of truth can change. It's your interpretation of truth that sets up your life.**

If you go your entire life believing something is true, it will change your thoughts, your decisions, and your actions.

There was a time people believed the earth was flat. When that was exposed as a lie, everything changed.

If you grew up believing that you were stupid … how did that change your thoughts?

If you grew up believing that you'd always be alone … how did that change your actions?

On the flip side -

Growing up believing that you're good enough to play basketball can change your future … ask Michael Jordan.

Growing up believing that you will experience a breakthrough can change your future …ask Einstein.

Growing up believing that you have something brilliant inside of you to bring to the world can change your future ... ask Steve Jobs.

It's your turn to decide the truth.

I'm not asking you to change your mindset — I'm asking you to examine your mindset to see if you want anything to change. Anytime you change your mindset, it will change your life. What you must begin to do is ask the question: What is true?

EXAMPLE RULE

If I am a barista at a local coffee shop, then I am not important.
(Oddly I know brilliant people that are baristas, and struggle with identity — feeling unimportant.)

As a barista, you will always feel unimportant unless you look deeper to ground yourself in reality. From your rule, decide what is truth and what is a lie.

FIND THE TRUTH.

(Physically list out what is true in this situation.)

  -My worth does not rest on the type of job I hold.
  -The way I treat the connections I make in my job (regardless of being a barista or a CEO) is what matters.
  -The person I am without money is a reflection of who I will be with money.

THIS ISN'T AN "ACTIVITY" — THIS IS A LIFESTYLE.

Finding and then grounding yourself in truth isn't just a concept. This is a process that you must do daily when you encounter a rule. You experience pain because of your beliefs. If you no longer want to be bound by the rule, you must find a more powerful truth to ground yourself in. It's not just a one time "activity" to think of truth. This is an ongoing process that you must remind yourself.

The next time you get triggered, stop. Acknowledge the rule then find the truth.

The truth process is not to be used as a justification for why or why not you do something. It is an opportunity to examine for yourself what is true.

Take your original rule and break it down to discern what is true and what is a lie. The purpose is to arrive at what is true so that you can begin to rest only on the truths.

Look at your Unwritten Rules through three different lens:
1. Yourself
2. Others
3. The Situation

When you break down the rule, look at the truth from three different perspectives — yourself, others and the situation as a whole.

1. What is true about yourself?
   Example: My intelligence exists independently of others perceptions.

2. What is true about the other people in the situation?
   Example: My boss can appreciate my hard work, even if he doesn't always take the time to tell me.

3. What is true about the situation as a whole?
   Example: Intelligence is not determined by a piece of paper.

Break down what is true regarding your rule so that you can begin to change your beliefs, which means the opportunity to change your future.

EVEN IF YOU ONLY GET THIS:

- Some things have seemed to be true for so long, people don't even question them.

- Breaking down truth is powerful to decide for yourself what you believe.

- Before you let your rules control the way you live — examine what is true about yourself, others, and the situation.

IF YOU STOP READING NOW,
YOU'LL MISS THIS:

Change can be difficult. It's difficult to cut something off from your life. Even things that are not healthy for us are tough to get rid of. In theory you would break a bad habit, but it is never that easy. The next chapter is about cutting off the lies so that you can replant truth.

CHAPTER 11

CUT OFF THE LIE.

CHOICES ARE SCARY.

You have the choice of what to believe.

Knowing that you are in control of your life can be terrifying. Here's proof: A friend of mine, Natalie, recently quit smoking. The craziest thing was that she had no problem quitting. Within a couple days, Natalie was amazed at how much better she felt and at how much time she had. All of a sudden, Natalie could see how she was in control of her own life. She realized she had the power to change things that were hurting her. That's exciting, right?

Well ... it freaked Natalie out.
It overwhelmed her and made her feel sick that this entire time she had the ability to change her situation.

> *" Our deepest fear is not that we are inadequate,*
> *but that we are powerful beyond measure. "*

MARIANNE WILLIAMSON

I wonder how often we, too, get overwhelmed by our own ability to change things. It scares us. It makes us realize how many missed opportunities we've had in the past.

Accountability is not easy. It means you bear the weight that you are in control of your life. It means that every choice matters - and you know it. Yet, most people would rather continue to operate in the default pattern* of what is easy.

[*Default Pattern: actions we take without awareness because they are our default decisions]

You have the choice.
The choice of what you believe and what you act on.
You have the choice to either accept the rule or separate yourself from the rule.
Now that you have identified your truth, it's time to separate yourself from the lies.

[*IF* TRIGGER ,

THEN DEEPEST FEAR .]

[Just because TRIGGER] it does not mean [you are your DEEPEST FEAR].

Separate who you are from external circumstances you have let define you.

Your value as a human being is not conditional.
It's not determined by what you do or what you've done.
It's not determined by what you have or what you don't.
It's not determined by what you said or what you thought.

Do you believe you should feel bad about yourself if [TRIGGER]?
If you aren't the most athletic on the court?
If you can't cook anything more advanced than chicken with some flavoring?
If you didn't get the promotion?

Your dreams and goals can be pursued. You can strive to do bigger things. You can measure yourself by the pursuit of your values and desires, but your worth as a human being does not depend on it.

Your worth is inherent.
Where is your worth at risk?

This is one of the most crucial pieces in identity:
Knowing that no matter what you do, how badly you screw up, you will still have as much value as the next person.

When you can see this, you can separate your rules from who you are.
You can separate a one time external event, that you may or may not have been able to control, from how you value yourself. Otherwise, it is dangerous when you define yourself by your rules.

DON'T PUT YOUR RULES ON ME.

Whether people say it, or people imply it through their actions, they are imposing truths on your life. In fact, they already have. (Sometimes even with good intention.)

"Running for office is what you were put on this earth to do."

People will claim things for you. Something that may seem like a compliment, can end up destructive when your external circumstances change. What if you don't get elected for office? What if you don't get re-elected? What if you desire to be a writer instead?

You must know who you are and who you are not. **If you don't know who you are, others will tell you who you should be.** You must protect yourself from the rules of others. The first step to doing this is being able to separate who you are from the rule itself.

"Oh, you haven't had kids yet ... "
"Why are you dating her?"
"You should get a real job..."

I've had people make fun of me for eating healthy. It happens quite a bit actually. Even when I pursue opportunities of growth in my life, people around me try to question my actions and make me feel bad. (Mind you, the rules of others usually come from a place of their own insecurity. People that challenge me on eating healthy usually have their own struggles around food or weight.)

You must be clear on who you are, or you are in danger of being influenced by the rules of others.

While it's important to surround yourself with people that will push and challenge you — changing your influences also means setting boundaries to protect yourself from influences that do not deserve that place in your life. The key here is knowing how to separate yourself from the rules others give you. When you see other people trying to force their rules on you, call it out when you see it. Whether you acknowledge what's happening in your head, or out loud, separate yourself from taking on these new rules.

Armor up and protect yourself from the rules of others.
You must learn to do this; your sanity and growth depend on it. You must learn to separate yourself from the rules of others because even when people mean well, they still put their Unwritten Rules on you.

SEPARATE YOURSELF FROM THE LIES.

Accept the rule — the trigger and the identity question — then admit it does not define you. To separate who you are means you must draw a line.

TRIGGER does not equal DEEPEST FEAR.

You might feel a certain way, but you are not *less*.
You might feel like a failure…
You might feel unimportant…
You might feel alone…

But your worth does not change.

You are not IDENTITY GAP, even if TRIGGER.
One thing alone cannot dictate who you are. Your value is not contingent on one circumstance or one trigger.

As you seek to impact people — and provide value to the lives of others — you MUST know your value. This is one of the hardest things, to come to a place where your value cannot be taken from you.
Your value cannot waiver based on one event.
Your value cannot waiver based on one fight.
Your value cannot waiver based on one ignored text message.
Your value cannot waiver based on one look.

Your value cannot waiver based on your income.

Your value cannot waiver based on a test score.

Identity is as much about who you are as it is about who you are not.
Know who and what you are not.

DECLARE THAT YOU ARE NOT DEFINED BY YOUR RULES.

I want to be clear, this isn't just talk. It's not just saying words out loud. There has to be an internal conviction that you are not defined by your rules. It's simultaneously a verbal and emotional shift in perspective. When you declare it, something moves inside of you. One easy way to do this is immediately call out (in your head, or heck, even out loud):

"I am not IDENTITY GAP."

Even though I just made a huge mistake…

I am not a failure.

I am not stupid.

"I am not defined by TRIGGER."

I am not defined by losing a game of volleyball.

I am not defined by other people's expectations of me.

When you recognize that you've been triggered and you see it's threatening your identity, you must cut it off right there before it begins to fester and makes things worse.

Your value goes with you wherever you go. If you lack value here, it will always stay with you. Your lack of self-value will influence everything you pursue. If you operate with this hole in your identity, you are operating from a place of need. How can you help others when you are constantly seeking your own need? How can you be good for others when you are constantly seeking to feel validated?

Purpose is an *overflow* of knowing your value. It is not the means for you to fill a hole of never ending pain.

You must move to a place where your value is unconditional. (This isn't an end result — it's a constant movement in this direction.) I once read, the best way to determine someone's future success is not to look at where they are, but look at where they are facing.

Which way are you facing?

Do you still find yourself sitting in the pain and and misery, trying to fill your internal hole?

OR

Are you living to pursue your truths and your values so that you can impact those around you?

It's not easy to get there. It's not easy to get to a place of knowing your worth. But there are a few things we can look at that will allow you to begin to separate who you are from your conditions.

EVEN IF YOU ONLY GET THIS:

- Most people operate in a default pattern and accept the rules they have received from the world.

- Be aware of the rules other people will try to put on you, even in good intention.

- When you take accountability of your rules, you no longer have to be defined by them.

- You can separate yourself from your deepest fear. If you don't separate yourself, your deepest fear will stay with you wherever you go.

> *Why it matters to Find Your Thing*
  When you get to a place of worth, you can live out purpose. Too many people are living out their thing, but lacking who they are. When you are not defined by your rules, you can live out your purpose in bigger ways.

IF YOU STOP READING NOW,
YOU'LL MISS THIS:

There is a Ted Talk called "The Stories We Tell Ourselves." It illustrates reality is simply a reflection of the stories we tell ourselves. The story is about a small boat crew stranded in the middle of water with only two options to get to land.

Option 1: The longest route. However, the crew doesn't have enough food to survive so it is highly unlikely they would make it.

Option 2: The shortest route. However, there are rumored cannibals along the way.

Which option would you choose? The crew chose the longer route because of the overwhelming fear of cannibalism. Cannibalism was more terrifying than the fear of just dying from not making it to shore.

Oddly enough, the crew did not make it and ended up resorting to cannibalism among one another to try to save themselves.

Decisions are based on the meaning that has been attached to certain things. If cannibalism is unthinkable in your minds, then you will take the longer route because there are cannibals.
When it comes time to make a decision, people decide based on the stories they tell themselves.
You must look deeper at the stories you tell yourself so that you can redefine the meaning.

CHAPTER 12

REWRITE YOUR STORY.

THIS IS WHERE THE TRUE POWER OF THE BOOK COMES IN.

You must learn to rewrite the meaning, or you will be stuck in what has already been defined for you.

WHEN "TRAGEDY STRIKES."

The world tells you what something means.

They tell you that it's tragic IF …

  you have a child before you are married.

  you are divorced .

  you are still single at age 35.

  you are overweight.

  you don't have any kids or grandkids.

 … then you are a failure.

Many times we take on the world's meaning without getting to decide for ourselves.

I'M SORRY.

If you lose your job, there is an auto response by people.

"I'm sorry."

Who says you have to feel bad when you lose a job? Why can't losing your job be a thing to celebrate? Jon Acuff, a writer that I really enjoy, talks about how the world said "I'm sorry" when he lost his job. He began to question, why did losing his job have to be a bad thing, when it actually ended up changing his life for the better?

What are other things society tells us is tragedy? What are the things society says that should be celebrated?

Even the people closest to us can force their meaning on our lives. Check your text messages, your Facebook posts, or just listen in to your conversations. People tell us what to feel good about and what to feel bad about. What are your friends, family, and other influences in your life saying is tragic? What are they telling you is worth celebrating?

I want to be clear that you do not need to see the positive in everything. (That is false optimism.) However, I am telling you to think independently of what everyone else is saying or doing. **We often limit ourselves when we let other people tell our story.**

CHANGING THE MEANING OF YOUR TRIGGER ... TO CHANGE YOUR IDENTITY.

Redefine meaning.
The meaning already exists ... somewhere in your head the meaning has been constructed by outside influences in one way, shape, or form.

This is not an opportunity to remove accountability from yourself.
It's actually the opposite. You are becoming accountable for everything in life. Although you can't control circumstances, you can control your choices.

Let's talk about the process of meaning making as it originated, by looking at a snake. There are two elements of meaning that are important to look at.
1. Inherent Meaning: No matter what we do or think, a snake will always slither. It will always need to eat. It may always be certain colors. We do not control this part of how we see a snake.

2. Adopted Meaning: There is an element of a snake's meaning that humans create. You get to dictate what a snake means to you. You can decide that snakes are scary and run the other way or kill them. You can decide that snakes are friendly and should be training and protected. Whether it be from your own experiences or the stories you have heard, adopted meaning exists in all areas of life.

If you don't like the rule you created — rewrite it.

[*IF* I DON'T GET THE PROMOTION , *THEN* I'M NOT SUCCESSFUL .]

If you are currently defining success based on whether or not you get the promotion, when you don't get the promotion, it will crush your soul if you don't rewrite that rule.

Consciously remind yourself that you get to define success. You get to define your rules.

How will you define success? Is it about a title? Is it about chasing your dreams? Is it about having a family? Is it about failing 100 times just to make it that one time? Is it about growth?

People have their own reality of what it means to be:
Successful
Important
Happy
Courageous

Again, you define the meaning. Each person has their own definition of these words, but not always because they made a conscious decision to define the meaning. Many of these words have been tainted by the world, before you even got here. And if the words weren't already tainted enough, society and the people around you continue to create new meaning for these words.

Rewrite your own definition. Rewrite your own meaning. When you rewrite your meaning, you are no longer a slave to the word, but you are free to pursue what matters to you.

THE RISK: CARRYING AROUND THE WEIGHT WITH YOU FOREVER.

If I work a job that pays 20K, I am a failure.

Failure.

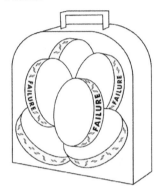

Do you want to carry around the title "failure?" Do you want to carry "failure" around with you on your pursuit to make $200,000 or $2,000,000? Do you want to carry "failure" home with you to your wife and kids after a long day of work? Do you want to carry "failure" around when you are hanging with your friends on a friday afternoon?

You may not be able to control outside influences, but you can control your response.

What if you had the ability to separate who you are from the title of failure?

REDEFINE THE MEANING OF YOUR SITUATION.

What does it mean to you to work a job that pays 20K?

Does it have to mean failure? What if it means ...

You are pursuing your dream. You were initially pursuing a career path that your family laid out for you, and it was never something you wanted in the first place. In fact, your 20K job, is the first opportunity you've had in the last 15 years with the flexibility for your dream.

You are a good father. Maybe for the last five years you have only invested in yourself and moving up the ladder and that was miserable. You neglected your wife and your three young kids. Now this job is an opportunity to reconnect to what matters.

You are moving up. Maybe you're making more than you ever have in your life, which accounts for the growth that you've experienced over the last few years.

How you see your situation changes everything. Even if you hate everything about your job — and hate making 20K — do you still want to own the title of failure? Do you really think that is who you are and what you deserve to be labeled? You can feel worthless when *they* tell you to, or you can define the meaning for yourself.

PERSONAL STORY OF MEANING.

I wrote the passage below a few years back and put it in here so you could see the reality of *why* we must identify rules and then smash through them.

"The last two years have been the most difficult years of my life. Now that this season is coming to an end, I would not change any of it for the world because it brought me greater perspective and great growth. It was during this time that I had to ask myself these questions of worth. I had to ask myself the question, 'Do my circumstances dictate my worth?' 'Do people have the freedom to tell me how I should feel about the things in my life?'"

When I was experiencing struggle a few years back, I could have let that define me. I could have accepted defeat. It's only after the fact that we often rewrite the meaning. But why not before? Why not rewrite the meaning from the beginning?

I had to rewrite my rules and I am still rewriting my rules. I had to fight the battles of identity back then and I am still fighting the battle of identity. I am thankful to say, society does not get to tell me the meaning for my life. Only I get to choose what is meaningful. The same is true for you.

This is why people love inspirational stories of people who lost an arm or a leg and "came back" to do amazing things. Someone that was thought to never be able to walk again, and then becomes a triathlete champion is empowering. These are stories of people that rewrote the rules society gave them. Rewriting rules is empowering. Guess what? You can rewrite your rules too.

We celebrate the person with no arms or no legs that did amazing things because they rewrote the rules, but the funny thing is, why was greatness not expected from the beginning?

Why do we only rewrite rules after the fact?

To accomplish more than what has been laid out for your life, you must rewrite the rules.

The triathlete had to rewrite his own rules because as much as he might have wanted, other people will not rewrite them for him.

You must begin to tell society who you really are. You must write your own story.

If you do not write your own story, others will write it for you. In fact, they already have.

I am giving you permission to decide your own meaning, because whoever decided the meaning in the first place was no one more special than you. Just a human or two, probably a long time ago.

You can begin to do this in two simple ways. Rewrite the past or rewrite the present ... both of which will rewrite the future.

REWRITE THE PAST.

Rewriting your rules can be done by looking at the past. Take a look at some of the most influential moments in your life. What do these experiences and events mean to you? The way you translate the meaning of these will have a clear impact on how you see yourself in the future.

Are your past events worth rewriting?
Is there a different way you'd like to tell that story? (If you rewrote the story, how would that change your future?)

REWRITE THE PRESENT.

Look at some of the events in your life. Look around at what you are seeking and what you appear to be missing. How are you translating the meaning of your circumstances?

Are your present events worth rewriting?
Is there a different way you'd like to tell that story? (If you rewrote the story, how

would that change your future?)

There will always be rules. It's not about the rules that exist now — it's about what rules exist before the day is over.

Rewrite your rules; rewrite your future.

EVEN IF YOU ONLY GET THIS:

- If you don't write your story, someone else will.

- In fact, someone else already has declared your story.

- Instead of letting them decide, why don't you decide? They might have beat you to it, but what matters is that you define it now

IF YOU STOP READING NOW,
YOU'LL MISS THIS:

What would you bleed for ... fight for ... die for?
The words "purpose" and "passion" can be overused. These words are so overused that they begin to lack true meaning. When you go to the etymology of a word, you can understand the original intent.

You want to Find Your Thing ... your purpose ...
your passion ...

The word "passion" roots back to suffering. The etymology of passion references Christ's suffering on the cross. Christ bled for humanity.

What would you bleed for?

When you look at what someone would bleed for, you are looking at the serious depths – the core – of a human. At your core you will find both pain and purpose. Your deepest fear and your deepest desire both stem from the core of who you are. It's easy to think purpose and pain are opposite, but they are so closely tied. In fact, most of decisions in life root back to both your fears and your values. In fact, your deepest fears are one of the most acurate ways to discover your deepest values.

The next section will bring to the surface your purpose that has existed all along.

SECTION 3

PURPOSE.

CHAPTER 13

"I WANT TO FIND MY THING."

"*I WANT TO BE LIKE JOE,*" SHE SAID.
"*Joe knows what he is passionate about and he is living it out. I want to find my thing.*"

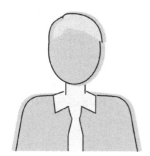

Joe is a local teacher and musician. He works day in and day out, doing everything he can to inspire inner city youth. Joe started a rap group, created his own non-profit and now he travels as a speaker to spread his message. People work with me for life coaching because they want to be like Joe. They have been out of college for a few years, jumped into an initial job or two, and now they sense there is more to life. They want to escape the monotony and do work that matters. They want to *find their thing* and they want to find it is as soon as possible.

When most people come to their first life coaching session, they are expecting to talk about passion. Instead we dive in immediately to what they hate – their deepest fear. (Just like you found your deepest fear in the first section.)

WHY YOU NEED TO KNOW YOUR DEEPEST FEAR:
People often confuse the pain of their deepest fear with a longing for purpose. Your deepest fear is your greatest pain. This pain has created a void inside of

you. Your void of identity is often misexplained as a longing for purpose. Oddly, people chase this fear, in hopes it will lead to purpose. Chasing a fear isn't what leads you to purpose, chasing the value behind purpose will lead you there. There is a distinct difference. Here's the secret: **Purpose does not come from chasing your fear. In fact, making decisions from a place of fear is dangerous.**

Do you think that Joe decided to pursue his work because of his deepest fear? Do you think that Joe works with youth because he is afraid he isn't good enough? Do you think Joe is looking for a group of inner city kids to tell him that he's *worth* it?
Joe's pursuit is not about the kids completing him. (Wouldn't that be weird if Joe's purpose was just about filling his own need?) Joe's desire is greater than him. Joe makes choices from an overflow of identity, knowing who he is, rather than running around town trying to find himself.

Joe moves for a greater reason of being. Joe has a unique value he is pursuing, not a fear he is running away from.

Don't miss this. Purpose does not come from scarcity. Purpose does not come from the emptiness of our insecurity. Purpose comes from the abundance of our values. To move to purpose, you must make the shift from focusing on the fear. Chasing a fear will lead you to remain empty; chasing a value is what leads to purpose.

You are well aware of your deepest fear - now begins the opportunity to see your greatest value so that you can live it out in your unique way.

Purpose:
Your unique way of living out your deepest value.

To *Find Your Thing* and live out purpose, you must discover your deepest value. Joe's life reflects his purpose - his unique way out living out his deepest value.

This is the shift that must happen before you get to your purpose. You must move from focusing on your deepest fear, to focusing on the pursuit of your greatest value.

Purpose is not a hole in your identity. Purpose is an overflow of your identity. An overflow is different than a hole. A hole means there is an absence; an overflow means there is an abundance. Joe operates from an overflow, rather than a hole in his heart. Do you see the difference?

This concept isn't about one person named Joe. Like Joe, you also have a greater reason for being. Your thing, your purpose, is greater than you. Purpose is not about filling your need, it's about fighting to fill the needs of others.

It's not your thing you need to find first, it's your purpose you need to pursue. Once you are living out purpose then you can choose your thing. You can't choose wrong when you are living out your greatest value in your unique way. Joe's life reflects his purpose — his unique way of living out his deepest value.

There is a shift that must happen before you get to your purpose.

Purpose is not a hole in your identity. Purpose is an overflow of your identity. An overflow is different than a hole. A hole means there is an absence, an overflow means there is an abundance. Joe operates from an overflow, rather than a hole in his heart. Do you see the difference?

This concept isn't about one person named Joe. Like Joe, you have a greater reason for being. Your *thing*, your purpose, is greater than you. **Purpose is not about filling your need, it's about fighting to fill the needs of others.**

It's not your thing you need to find first, it's your purpose. Once you have your purpose then you can *choose* your thing. You can't choose wrong when you are living out your greatest value in your unique way.

You'll know you've landed on purpose when you uncover your greatest value and then start start to pursue it in your unique way.
You started with a trigger.

TRIGGER > DEEPER FEAR > DEEPEST FEAR (THE HOLE IN YOUR IDENTITY)

Now that you have found your deepest fear, it is time to use that fear to reveal your purpose. Here is the next part of the journey:

DEEPEST FEAR > DEEPEST VALUE > PURPOSE > FIND YOUR THING

Now that you have access to your deepest fear, you can also access purpose.

EVEN IF YOU ONLY GET THIS:

- People claim to be pursuing purpose, but truthfully they are just running around trying to fill the void of their greatest fears and insecurities.

- Purpose is an overflow of who you are, not an absence.

- Purpose must come before your thing. To get to purpose, uncover your greatest value, and then pursue it in your unique way.

> *Why it matters to Find Your Thing*
Once you have your deepest fear, you can use it to *Find Your Thing*.

DEEPEST FEAR > DEEPEST VALUE > PURPOSE > FIND YOUR THING

IF YOU STOP READING NOW,
YOU'LL MISS THIS:

The strategy to finding your purpose is similar to the winning strategy for the game Operation™. Tweezers are used to pull objects out of the human body. On the surface, the game of Operation™ appears simple, yet each item must be pulled out of a tiny hole, without the tweezers even tapping the game board. Although it can be tempting to just jump right in and pull the wrench out of the ankle, if you move carelessly, the game buzzer will go off and you'll lose your turn. The game is difficult and practice alone is stressful. It takes patience and focus. It takes skill and strategy.

If pulling a plastic wrench out of a child's game is difficult ... imagine how difficult it is to pull purpose out of yourself. Purpose, like the game Operation™, must be approached with strategy and extreme precision.

To find the deeper value of purpose, you must be focused. You can't just wake up one day and expect to stumble on your purpose. To find your purpose, you must carefully dissect your life to get to the core. Purpose exists at the core of who you are. The core of who you are does not just contain one answer or one purpose. At the core of who you are, you can find anything that matters to you. This is the place that influences your thoughts, your decisions, and your motivations. It contains both your values and your fears, and therefore also your deepest pain.

You have found the core by understanding your deepest fear. Now the opportunity exists to pull out your purpose from the same place.

DEEPEST FEAR> DEEPEST VALUE > FIND YOUR THING

CHAPTER 14

THE DOUBLE EDGED SWORD
OF PURPOSE.

WHAT YOU FOCUS ON BECOMES YOUR REALITY

Have you ever seen a child play with a box?
Parents, family members and friends shower
their kids with birthday gifts, only to find them
spending the next two hours playing with the
cardboard box.

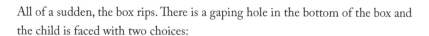

As a child starts to play, the box suddenly
comes alive. In the eyes of a child, the box
becomes a house or a car or a plane. In that
moment, there is no greater gift. The possibilities are endless.

All of a sudden, the box rips. There is a gaping hole in the bottom of the box and
the child is faced with two choices:

Choice #1: Focus on the problem.
The child can cry and run around furiously, trying to patch up the hole, only to
be indefinitely disappointed that his new found toy will never be the same again.

Choice #2: Use the hole as a new opportunity.
Rather than sitting in misery and complaining that there is something wrong

with the cardboard gift, most kids will find new opportunities.

The *hole* quickly becomes a window to see out of the imaginary house. Then it becomes a dashboard to fly the plane into the sky.

What started out as enjoyable could have become a tragedy. The defective box remained better than any other gift because the child shifted to see the opportunity.

Here you are, sitting with a similar hole — a hole in your identity. This is your insecurity that often harms yourself and those around you. Your deeper fear has been in your life, creating pain for yourself and others. Some people would say your insecurity is that part that makes you defective. You may have always known your fear was there, but this time, you see a choice.

Just like the child finds a new opportunity with the box, there is another opportunity for you.

Choice #1: Focus on your deepest fear.
You can cry and run around furiously, trying to patch up the hole, only to be indefinitely disappointed that things will never be the same again.

Most people dwell in the pain. They choose to focus on their deeper fear. When you focus on pain, you severely limit your opportunities. Your deepest fear will control your decisions and your life.

Are you choosing to let your deepest fear control your life?

When you feel hurt, it's hard to see anything else. It's hard to even think about other opportunities.

Choice #2: Use your deepest fear as an opportunity.
The opportunity comes when you shift from focusing on your deeper fear to your greater value.

This option is much more difficult. It requires awareness, accountability and action. However, the joy at the other end is much greater.

YOU DID THE WORK TO FIND YOUR DEEPEST FEAR, NOW WHAT?

Like you, John did the work in section two to find his deepest fear. John has a fear of being lost in life. His deepest fear is that he doesn't belong.

When John and I first spoke, he had a lot going on in his life. He wasn't doing well in his job and was confused about whether or not to end a long term relationship. The events in John's life left him feeling confused and unsure of what he wanted. Feeling lost made John feel horrible on the inside. It started with the Unwritten Rule: *If I'm not doing well in my job, then I'm lost.* After looking deeper, and doing the work in section two, John realized: *If I'm lost, then I don't belong.* His deepest fear was lack of not belonging.

What you don't know about John is that his friends look up to him. For years, people have come to John for answers because he was the only one that seemed to have direction in his life. While most of his friends felt stuck, John always had answers on how to take the next step. In fact, John was paid full time to help other people with direction in their life.

The very thing John was trying to help others with, he was now struggling with himself. How can this be?

How can the thing John is terrified of be the same thing that he helps other people with?

Can you be good at helping others with something and still be stuck on it yourself?

Yes.

Your deepest fear is strongly connected to one of your deepest values.

John's deep fear of being lost is correlated with his desire to help others escape the misery of being lost. This is the same shift you now have the opportunity to make.

Do you see that?
Fear = Lost
Value = Belonging

SHIFT FROM FEAR TO VALUE.

John had two choices.
Choice #1: Focus on the pain of feeling lost.
Choice #2: Focus on the value of belonging.

Some days John chooses the pain of feeling lost. He beats himself up because he hates feeling that way. Other days, John is inspired to help other people fight through their pain.

John never realized his deepest fear was so strongly connected to one of his greatest values.

It is a choice. What you choose to focus on becomes your reality.
Life changes when you shift focus away from your deepest insecurity and onto your deepest desire.

THE DOUBLE EDGED SWORD.

Are you familiar with a double edged sword? One situation can have both a good and a bad outcome. With every benefit, there is the possibility for risk. The same weapon that can advance you, can also defeat you. One of the most empowering realizations is that your insecurity of identity can also lead you directly to your purpose. John's fear of being lost can leave him defeated or lead him to conquer. John's deeper fear is also a gift—because of his fear, John has an increased ability to fight for others that feel lost.

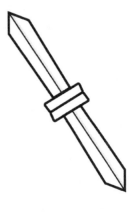

Your greatest fears aren't just empty fears, they are strongly linked with your greatest values.
Your fears connect to your values. This is the double edged sword. A double edged sword is powerful. A double edged sword means that even amongst your pain, an opportunity always exists for you to advance and slay.

How is that possible?

How can the place of deep pain also be a place of great strength? The power comes when you turn over the sword. This is the shift. Recognize your fear and then see the value on the other side.

People often limit themselves to an either/or mentality. Pain and purpose seem opposite—therefore people are taught to run from pain. The true gift of purpose is experienced among pain.

What is your deepest fear? (If you forgot, reference back to section two.)

Make the shift for yourself. Flip the sword away from your deepest fear to identify the value on the other end. What do you see?

What is your greatest value?

The goal of this chapter is to move from drowning in your fears to living for your values. Too often people get stuck. Understanding your values moves you to purpose. Purpose is your unique ability to live out your greatest value. Take a moment to get clear on what you see as your greatest value.

Unsure of your greatest value? Identify a value for now. You will have the opportunity to refine this value later.

NEEDING LOVE VS. LOVING:
Children who have horrible parents often grow up questioning, "Am I loved?"

Kyle grew up carrying the deeper fear of being unlovable. It's not a coincidence that because the powerful fear of being unlovable also presents his greatest value.

Kyle grew up with horrible parenting. He could spend his time dwelling in pain and feeling horrible, but instead he spends it helping people feel loved.

Deeper Fear: Not being loved
Deeper Value: Loving

There is the always a choice. Some people choose to stay in fear their entire life, and others make the shift to see and pursue the value. There is the always the choice. Some people choose to stay in fear their entire life, and others, make the shift to see and pursue the value. More specifically, Kyle does everything he can to help others be good parents. Purpose comes out through Kyle as he finds ways to specifically use his unique value. He writes, he speaks, and he lives it daily to inspire other parents.

UNSEEN VS. SEEING OTHERS:

One of the most influential people I know, Eric, grew up unseen in school. Eric could have stayed bitter. Eric could have lived life with a chip on his shoulder, feeling unworthy because he never had teachers that fought for him. Instead, he decided to flip the sword. Eric has spent the last 25 years fighting for high students to be seen. He moved to the value.

Deeper Fear: Unseen (Being a Nobody)
Deeper Value: Seeing people (Helping them feel known)

The double edged sword of fear and value exist in so many areas of life - the difference is the choice to use the pain to see opportunity. Eric steps into a greater reason for existence when he pursues the value, and the power comes when he pursues it in the unique way that only he can. Everyone that was unseen doesn't need to be a teacher. In fact, Eric's purpose isn't limited to teaching. Eric's uniqueness comes as he challenges others and calls out their unseen potential.

INSIGNIFICANT VS. CREATING SIGNIFICANCE:

One of my clients, Jenna, was struggling to feel significant. Jenna constantly found herself frustrated when her friends didn't appreciate her. In her second life coaching session, Jenna told me about a birthday event she was planning for herself over text message with her friends. Jenna was hurt. She didn't understand. Her friends didn't really seem excited about Jenna's birthday, and weren't responding back to the text messages. Jenna felt like they didn't care. She felt like they didn't appreciate her. This wasn't a one-off situation. Jenna realized at work she often felt insignificant when her coworkers didn't seem to notice her greatness.

Deeper Fear: Insignificance
Deeper Value: Significance

Jenna originally fixed her eyes on the pain and the fear. It felt horrible to be treated as though she didn't matter. But, instead of dwelling in the pain, Jenna made the shift to see her value. While Jenna knew that she was good at making others feel significant, she didn't realize a lot of that gift came because of her own painful experiences. Jenna made the shift away from fear by embracing her unique value of significance. She flipped the double edged sword.

Remember, purpose isn't about running away from something but running toward something. Purpose is running toward a value.

What value are you running toward?
If you haven't already, look back at the hole in your identity (your deepest fear), and flip the sword. What is at the other end? What is one of your greatest values?

RESPECT.

Deeper Fear: Are you are triggered daily when people treat you disrespectfully and you cannot imagine a greater feeling than receiving respect at work, at home, and with your friends?

Deeper Value: You likely have the unique ability to bring respect wherever you go. Regardless of where someone comes from, how they speak or who they hang out with, you take love and respect to new levels.

ENCOURAGEMENT.

Deeper Fear: Have you been dying to be supported and encouraged by others?
Deeper Value: While you can't seem to get encouragement from anyone around you, you have the ability to give it like no other.

RECOGNITION.

Deeper Fear: Have you been hoping to be recognized for your achievements and accomplishments?
Deeper Value: It's likely the greatest gift you have is the ability to see that in others.

IMPACTING OTHERS.

Deeper Fear: Is your deepest fear that you are living life without impacting others?

Deeper Value: While you've been beating yourself up day in and day out, feeling like you have yet to do anything of impact, you are probably missing the power behind your desire to help others impact the world.

MAKE THE SHIFT FROM FEAR TO VALUE.

True purpose doesn't stem from your desire to fill a hole of identity, nor does it stem from your desire to feel whole. Purpose exists in the space where you look to fill the holes of others — when you look to make others whole.

Now you are finally seeing your deepest fear for the greater capacity it holds.

You didn't realize that your deepest fear is one of your greatest values? The fact that your fear pains you so much is a sure sign that it matters to you. This is what it means to switch from your fear, to embracing your value.

The place where you suffer most is the place where you have the ability to see the suffering of others. Where do you see suffering in the world? It likely originated because you were susceptible to the same suffering. People separate pain and pleasure. They seem opposite and yet the truth is, internal pain and pleasure are often rooted in the same place.

What moves you comes from the core of who you are. What brings you the greatest joy has the ability to cause you the greatest pain. Think about anything that matters to you. Most people have a deep love for their family. If family matters to you, it also has the ability to cause you the greatest amount of pain. Looking at your greatest fears allows you insight to the things that matter most.

Remember, there is always the choice.

Choice #1: Tirelessly chase your deeper fear. You can run around trying to beg others to fill your deepest insecurity. (This is like an invisible target–you can never really catch it.)

Choice #2: Make the shift. Use the opportunity of your fear as a fresh lens to see your value. While your insecurity is unique to you, so are your values and your purpose. You have the ability to see the world from a fresh perspective; take it.

DEEPEST VALUE > PURPOSE > FIND YOUR THING

FIND YOUR THING.

The word *find* means to "discover something valuable." You did it. You discovered something valuable. You took your deepest fear and landed on a greater value.

EVEN IF YOU ONLY GET THIS:

- The same fear that has the power to destroy you can actually be used for greater purpose.

- Are you on the brink of defeat because you don't feel significant? Significance is likely one of your greatest gifts.

- As much as you want others to fill your deepest insecurities — they won't.

- Instead of running around, forever stuck in pain, you can use that same place to live out your purpose.

- Purpose exists when you move beyond the hole in your heart and look to fill the holes of others.

> *Why it matters to Find Your Thing*
> If you want to *Find Your Thing*, you won't find it by hanging around in your fears all day. You must actively move from your fears to your values.

IF YOU STOP READING NOW,
YOU'LL MISS THIS:

Translation does not have to be word for word.
My family and I were visiting New York where we met a family of
three from China; A mom, dad, and an eight year old boy. Like us,
our new friends appeared to be roaming around New York City on a
hot day in July. In total, this Chinese family probably spoke roughly
30 words of English. Throughout our short interaction, I learned that
the boy's name was Steven. Steven and his family were in line with us
to take the boat to Ellis Island. As we went through security, I looked
back and saw Steven and his family held up. The security officers
were trying to communicate to the family regarding their bag, but
Steven and his family just looked confused.

I went over to investigate. And as I was walking up, the
officer managed to get the father to open the bag and reveal the
contents inside.

The prized possessions that this family had been toting around New
York City for hours in their son's school backpack contained a measly
nine cans of their favorite, Asian, lukewarm beer.

After recovering from my fit of laughter, I realized they needed help.
These silly officers were obviously not getting through to this family
with their loud english, "NO BEER!"

So I took it upon myself to intervene with my own translation. I
stepped up to the plate and clearly said, "NO BEER!" but added a
very effective hand gesture that managed to get the point across. The
family innocently nodded and complied, left the beer, and boarded
the boat.

The officers were amazed.

Wait, what just happened? My family witnessed this whole charade and laughed at my efforts the entire time. I stepped in with so much certainty believing that I could translate for this family, even though I could not speak a word of Chinese.

Sometimes translation is more than a direct transfer of words. It's knowing how to "translate" that counts.

Most things in life translate to your values. In the last chapter you discovered that even your deepest fears lead to values.

The next chapter will teach you how to translate your past decisions, your present thoughts, and your future desires into your purpose.

CHAPTER 15

PURPOSE CONNECTS YOUR PAST, YOUR PRESENT, & YOUR FUTURE.

CHILDREN DREAM ABOUT HAVING SUPERPOWERS.
Some kids dream of flying, others want to be invisible. I always liked the idea of mind reading. Sometimes mind reading is easier than you think. Spend five minutes with a person and you can learn so much. You might even learn things about someone that they have not even admitted to themselves.

People will tell you everything you want to know about them, you just have to listen. Listen to what people say, and more importantly, listen to what they don't say. The same is true for you.

READ YOUR OWN MIND.

Have you ever thought about the power to read your own mind?
You aren't hard to read. Who you are is not a foreign concept. Listen to yourself. Watch yourself. What are you saying? What are you not saying? What are you doing? What are you not doing? Clarity has always been there.

It sounds silly, and yet, many times people aren't aware of their own thoughts and desires. Just like people lack awareness of their pain, most people lack awareness of what they truly value.

Reading your mind is the key to purpose. Your purpose is not a new thing; it's not a new idea. Purpose has always existed because it's who you are. It's not a thing. It's bigger than a thing. It's a culmination of everything. Your past and your present and everything in between. In the same way, your purpose is connected in every aspect of life. If you look at what you say and what you do, it's easy to understanding your purpose. Purpose is often just lost in translation.

Translation is easy if you know what you're doing. I'm going to show you how to translate what you are saying and what you are doing to your greatest values, so that you can see your purpose.

LEARN TO READ YOUR MIND SO THAT YOU CAN ...

1. CLAIM YOUR GREATEST VALUES.

Lay your stake in the ground. Making decisions isn't easy, especially when fear is present. Learn to center yourself on your deepest values as much as possible. Don't just become aware of your deepest value one time. Continuously bring your values top of mind to increase your odds of acting on them. (Really, it's a crazy concept, and yet without keeping your values top of mind, how can you expect to make decisions for them?) The truth is, fears always exist. The goal isn't getting rid of your fears. The goal is to pursue your deeper values *regardless* of the fear.

2. PURSUE YOUR VALUES IN YOUR UNIQUE WAY (PURPOSE)

Purpose, as defined in this book, is your unique way of living out your deepest value. Purpose is not passive. True purpose is pursued. You don't live in purpose simply by letting a series of decisions come to you. **Claim your values then claim ground with your values.** Purpose is about claiming ground with your values and living them out on your unique way.

Go through the next chapters with the intent of solidifying your deepest values and putting words to purpose — your unique way of living out your values.

TRANSLATE YOUR PAST DECISIONS.

Your choices tell all. If you dissect the most influential moments in your life, there you will see your values.

Life changing moments point to a decision in your life. The art of deciding is choosing what matters — choosing your value.

What have been some of your biggest life changing moments?

One of my biggest life changing moments was making the decision to go to college at Central Michigan University. Before that moment, my life was already planned for me. If you read the first couple chapters of the book, you'll know that in school, I graduated top of my class and was an overachiever at almost everything. Therefore, I was not only told, but it was expected, that I would go to a prestigious school. Growing up in Michigan, minimally that looks like going to the University of Michigan.

My senior year of high school, I made the decision to forgo the expectations that were set for me. Not only did I give up going to Michigan, but I actually chose a school that most people look down upon.

Choice: Choosing Central Michigan

Value: Deciding my college independently of others expectations

Deepest Value: Pursuing a life that is not limited by the world's expectations

It is powerful to know what you value. The only thing more powerful than knowing what you value is taking one moment to understand how it connects to your purpose. The question is: How do you uniquely live out your greatest value? (Note: Diving in to the uniqueness of your value will be covered in the next chapter.)

A deeper value in your life will come up in many places.

It's not a coincidence that other life changing moments also equate to this value. Not being defined by others is a value that has continued to come up in my life.

When I was coming close to college graduation, my life was again lined up by the expectations of those around me. I planned to go into higher education. Because of my college resume, I would not only get a great salary, but would have my masters degree, housing, and food all paid for the next two years. Instead of doing what was lined up and expected, I took a risk. I decided to go all in to build a nonprofit we had started four years back. I didn't know how I was going to make money but I know that it was important to me. Hence, again, I made the decision to operate from the value of not being defined by others.

When you break down the life changing moments in your life, it is likely they connect directly to the thing you value most.

What were the most life changing moments in your life?

What values do you see from your life moments?

Our past is connected to our purpose because it has shaped who we are. We grow from our past, or rather the moments we chose to grow from, shaped who we are and shaped what we care about. Our "AHA moments!" reveal our greatest values and in these values lies the pursuit of purpose.

All roads lead to purpose.

Every moment = a choice. What does that choice say about you?

TRANSLATE YOUR PRESENT THOUGHTS.

> *"If you want to know where your heart is, look to where your mind goes when it wanders."*
>
> ANONYMOUS

What are the thoughts currently sitting in your head. What are you spending time thinking about, worrying about, and frustrated around?

What are you currently spending time dwelling on? Don't overthink this part. Look at recent events this past week that brought about frustration.

EXAMPLE

Recently Chris has been spending a lot of time thinking about his relationship and how much that weighs on him. He feels a lot of negativity coming from his relationship and is starting to question, whether or not it's worth his time.

Value: Spending time with people that make him better

Deeper Value: Personal Growth

Even the things that seem to be frustrating still point to the values that matter most. The reason an experience is bothering you is because something about it matters. The question is, why? What about that experience matters to you?

If there is a fear, don't be afraid to acknowledge that first, to better understand the value.

EXAMPLE

Frustration: Kelsey's boss called her out in front of our team for not showing up on time to the meeting.

Fear: Disappointing others

Value: Not being a disappointment

Deeper Value: Showing people they are not a disappointment

When you encounter a moment of frustration, identify the root issue of your frustration to see what you value. The truth is, your thoughts are a reflection of your values.

TRANSLATE YOUR FUTURE DESIRES.

What are you longing for in the future?

Most people know they have dreams, but it's rare they think about the greater value they are pursuing behind the dream. Two people may have the same dream, but the power comes from knowing that person's deepest value.

Person #1:

Dream: Financial freedom

Value: Traveling with family

Deeper Value: Pursuing meaningful relationships

Person #2:

Dream: Financial freedom

Value: Having the ability to buy things for others

Deeper Value: Giving back to others

Your dreams point directly to what matters most, but the value comes when you know the reason why.

Your desires can also be rooted in your dissatisfaction. When you look beneath the fear, find the unbreakable value that matters to you.

Where are you currently unsatisfied in life?

Unsatisfied: Working 60 hours a week

Fear: Not having a life

Value: Freedom
Deeper Value: Meaningful Relationships
Some people work 60 hours a week and love it. Others work 60 hours a week and can't even look themselves in the mirror. If you're longing to work less hours, you can look deeper to find what you value.

All roads lead to purpose.
Your deepest value has power because it doesn't live in isolation.
It connects to everything. The power comes in seeing how it all connects.

Your past decisions, present thoughts, and future desires don't lie. They reveal your greatest values. They will never fail you. Don't miss them just because they are buried in your pain and in your fears. Most people are afraid of pain — they run away from it or allow it to destroy them. Even your frustrations and disappointments can be the greatest gift when you translate them to values.

DO NOT MOVE ON FROM THIS CHAPTER UNTIL YOU —

CLAIM YOUR TOP THREE GREATEST VALUES:

1.

2.

3.

(It's also helpful to define them. You may realize there is something more important.)

EVEN IF YOU ONLY GET THIS:

- Almost everything connects to your purpose, you just have to understand how to translate.

- Your past decisions, present thoughts, and future desires can all be translated to uncover your greatest values.

- Purpose isn't something you have to find; it has been with you all along.

> **Why it matters to Find Your Thing**
  Once you see how much of your life connects to your greatest values, you will have increased ability to see the capacity of your purpose.

IF YOU STOP READING NOW,
YOU'LL MISS THIS:

Have you ever participated in a cardboard boat race? You are timed to build the most sturdy boat as quickly as you can. Before the race, you look at your boat, and you are proud. It's likely everything you hoped and more. You think:
"Wow. This boat is amazing. There is no way I will sink."

All of a sudden, the race begins, you begin to paddle out your boat, when all of a sudden you realize, your boat is sinking.

This beautiful and indestructible boat outside of the water, didn't last more than 30 seconds inside of the water.

It did not withstand the true test.

You found one thing you really value.
Will it withhold the test?

In your head or on paper, you can say you have one thing, one value. Now let's see if it withholds the test as your greatest value.

If you put it out, will it sink?
If you drop it, will it break?

Throughout the next few chapters, we're going to continue to test your value to make sure it's not just the deepest value, but that it. Once you have your greatest value, you can live out your thing.

CHAPTER 16

UNIQUE & SPECIFIC.

GET SPECIFIC ON YOUR GREATEST VALUE.

There are two easy ways to never pursue purpose.

1. Focus on your fears. If you stay caught up in the pain, you'll never be able to move to your values. If you're this far in the book, you already know the power of your values. You have moved beyond just focusing on your pain.

2. Get caught up chasing too many surface values. Oftentimes the greatest barrier to pursuing your thing is that you are caught up in too many values.

When you say *"I want to impact everyone,"* you are flirting with saying, *"I want to impact no one."* Everyone is a dangerous word. It doesn't bring you to identify anyone.

When you say you want to help people in many ways, you risk impacting others in your unique way. If you don't identify someone or something that really matters, how will you ever pursue it?

Stepping into the uniqueness of your values isn't a new thing. When you look at your fears, your past, your present, and your future, what is the most important value? Where do they all align for a greater and more specific value? (Seriously, take a minute.)

WHAT ARE THE TOP THREE GREATEST VALUES YOU SEE IN YOUR LIFE?

1.

2.

3.

(It's also helpful to define them. You may realize there is something more important.)

WHICH OF YOUR VALUES IS THE MOST IMPORTANT?

(Note: There may be a theme that pulls them together. Many of your values root to one of the most important values.)

QUICK LITMUS TEST

1. Does it connect to your deepest fear?
2. Does it connect to your past decisions, present thoughts and future desires?

If the answer is yes, then you're probably spot on.

DO I NEED TO COMMIT TO ONE VALUE?

Yes. Commit to your greatest value as you look to define your purpose. It can always expand or change.

It's tempting to want to stay generic with your values. If I ask you, *"What's your purpose?"* most people will say, *"I love to help people."* If I ask you, *"How do you want to help people?"* most people stay vague until they eventually come back to, *"I just really want to help people."*

When you say *"I want to help people,"* it lacks specificity so much that it's hard to be in line to help anyone. Many people are so passionate about helping others that they don't want to be limited by just one thing. On the contrary, the most successful people I know are very good at focusing their energy. How do you want to help people? There isn't room to help everyone in every way. The people with the largest impact are laser focused on impacting in a specific way.

> *" People think focus means saying yes to the thing you've got to focus on. But that's not what it means at all. It means saying no to the hundred other good ideas that there are. "*
>
> STEVE JOBS

DEEPEST VALUE > PURPOSE

What is your unique gift to the world?
I remember when I was asked this question for the first time. It took me off guard. It's like I knew what it was, but I couldn't describe it. I will be honest, most people get confused here. They don't see a unique value in themselves. This is why you must first understand your greatest values. You have a unique gift. It connects with so much in your life.

You have a unique way of seeing the world. You have a unique way of helping people.

What is your unique way that you want to impact people with your greatest value?
You are unique. Your deepest fears are unique. Your greatest value can be pursued uniquely. If you want to *Find Your Thing*, you must get specific on your value. Simply "helping others" does not highlight your uniqueness. It does not highlight the uniqueness on how you can impact the world.

You'll know it aligns because it connects to your deepest fear, your past decisions, your present thoughts, and your future desires.

Many people value connection. Even if millions of other people value connection, you have a unique way of living out that value. You grew up differently. You have unique experiences. Valuing connection means something different to you than it does to someone else.

The more you can pinpoint what matters, the more you can describe it. The more you describe it, the more you can understand it. The more you can understand it, the more you will pursue it. Simplify and define your gift. Do not feel boxed in and limited, but be empowered by what matters to you.

In order to pursue the best, you have to stay focused on the best. You can't stay focused on everything. Put up some boundaries describing your unique way of living out your value. If you don't like your purpose, you can come back and knock down the boundaries later.

When you boil it down, what is the non-negotiable thing in your life that you want to pursue? Now, how do you uniquely live out this value?

DO NOT MOVE ON FROM THIS CHAPTER UNTIL YOU IDENTIFY YOUR PURPOSE:

What is the unique way you are pursuing your greatest value?

EVEN IF YOU ONLY GET THIS:

- Most people get caught up in chasing too many values, that they never pursue the greatest value.

- While it appears that you are centered because you want to help everyone, you actually miss out on the opportunity to deeply impact someone.

- What is your deepest value?

- The same value you want for yourself is likely the same value you bring to others.

CHAPTER 17

PURPOSE IS AN END, NOT A MEANS.

PURPOSE IS NOT THE MEANS, IT'S THE END.

When diving in to purpose, it's tempting to stay surface level. People often get caught up in the surface value, without understanding the true end of what they seek. The goal of this chapter is to look for greater depth in your value.

Purpose is not the means to the end; it's the end. If you want to know if you're pursuing purpose — ask yourself — am I pursuing the means or the ends?

So many people get caught up in the means, without understanding the end. What is the deeper thing you desire?

Let's look at two examples:
Steve. (His name isn't really Steve, but Steve is a fitting replacement name.)
Dave.

Steve came to me because he was eagerly looking for a new job, a new life. I remember the exact spot in Starbucks we sat for our coaching session.

> Steve: "Lisa, I need a new job. I need a job that has room to grow for me to make $80,000 a year."

<u>Me</u>: *"Okay, Steve. Are you sure that is what you need?"*

<u>Steve</u>: "Yes, I need a job that will make me 80K."

<u>Me</u>: *"Steve, why do you want a job that will make you $80,000 a year?"*

<u>Steve</u>: "I want to be generous. I want to be able to give money to people when they need it. I want to be able to buy people things when we go out for dinner or for coffee. Even $40,000 is good to start out with, as long as there is room to grow to 80K. I know that I can make my money spread further than most people. Trust me, I just know this will bring me the satisfaction I need."

Steve continued, "Lisa, I know I want money because I want to be generous. I want to transform the lives of people through generosity, but in order to do that, I need money. I want to pursue the things that will allow me the ability to make money. I need a new job."

Steve was unhappy with his current job and financial situation. Instead of just sitting around, he decided to invest his time and energy into changing it. I can't blame him. He did the right thing. Oftentimes, we are looking in the right direction for what we want, but are still a mile away from what really matters.

Maybe you're like Steve. You know you want something different. In fact, you think you know exactly what you want. A job that makes you $80,000 a year. That will solve all of your problems, right?

You can spend the next year pursuing the job you wanted more than anything in the world, only to realize, that was never your *true* desire. This is the result of a failure to explore the depth of your value. What is the truth *behind* your desire? Steve's new job was only the *means* to his endgame of generosity.

Before you get caught up in the means, what is your end desire?

Less than five months after this coaching session with Steve, Steve messaged me, *"Lisa, you were right."*

(Mind you, I never told Steve the new job he coveted was not the answer to his problems, but somehow, Steve realized the way I saw his desires.)

Steve was right. I *did* know that a job was not the answer to his problem. I knew Steve's fulfillment was not about a certain salary number. The depth of Steve's value was about generosity. Steve wanted to be a man that is generous.

What is the value that you are pursuing?

Is it a means or an end?

When you listen for the depth, what do you really want?

I want to stress that back when I first met with Steve, he would have argued with me for the rest of the week that making $80,000 a year was the only thing missing from his happiness. I also want to stress that Steve was intelligent, and also self-reflective, so realistically he should have been capable to see what he truly desired.

But it's not that easy.

To understand the actual desire of your heart, you must go below the surface. If it was easy, everyone would do it. It's not difficult, it just takes awareness and a few opportunities to practice. In this specific instance, Steve got caught up in the means. Simply put, he wanted fulfillment; he wanted to live a generous lifestyle. But instead of pursuing the life fulfilling generosity that he told me he wanted, he decided to pursue the means of an $80,000 salary.

Pursuing the "means" is not bad, just as long as you don't lose sight of the true end. Purpose is about pursuing an end.

How often do people miss what they truly desire because they focus on the means?

How often do people miss what matters because they search their brain for one *thing* that will answer all of their problems?

How would things change if people focused on pursuing the end result, rather than looking for a thing to fill the desire of purpose?

There are a million ways you can make 80K if that numeric value is important to you. Instead of keeping your eyes laser focused on the means, start with the end in mind.

What do you want to use the money for? What is your endgame?

Start with the end, *then* work back to the means.

If you don't start with the end, five months later you'll end up back to square one because you put your heart and soul into fighting for a false desire.

People are often living in means without giving a second thought to the end. For many, this isn't a monetary amount, but a relationship, a city, or a new endeavor. What is the deepest value behind your initial value? Why do you want to start that business? Move to Europe? Move out of your parents house? Break up with your girlfriend? Pursue that promotion?

Look at the deeper value you have landed on is this a means or an end?
Take a minute to translate your deepest value into an end.

Now, look at another example: Dave. Dave Ramsey and the successful organization he has created. Dave's program has a clear outline of steps you need to take to get out of debt. From what I have seen from afar, these steps are great and they work.

But don't forget the end. Don't forget the reason these steps exist.

Why do you desire to achieve financial independence in the first place?

Dave's model, oddly similar to Steve's value, is based on giving. Getting out of debt is important, with the end goal of being able to freely give to others. Keep your end result top of mind.
  Maybe your end goal is to enjoy life with your family.
  Maybe your end goal is to be able to travel the world indefinitely.
  Maybe your end goal is to be able to support your parents so they never have to work another day in their life.

We often get so wrapped up in the means that we lose sight of *why* it matters. It's easy to do this with money. People pursue money as a means to something, but in the process forget what they are pursuing. Money itself is only fulfilling when there is something greater. What is behind your desire to be a billionaire? Some people are weird about money, some people love money. The most important thing about money is the greater value that lies behind your pursuit of money.
  Maybe it's the freedom to never have to work again.
  Maybe it's the flexibility to do what you want, when you want.
  Maybe it's the power to give.
  Maybe it's the status and respect.
  Maybe it's the feeling like you are finally good enough.
  Maybe it's the productivity that comes from hiring others to help you with work.
Look at the end value, rather than the fear. What are you truly running toward?

It's important to know the deeper reason for your desires — the end behind the means. I like to call this your why — your purpose.

If your goal of making money is to give to others then don't miss the opportunities to give in the day to day. Don't miss the opportunity to give in the smaller things, just because "money is tight."

If your goal of making a million dollars is to be able to spend time enjoying your family, keep this in mind when one of your kids needs you for five minutes. (Yes, even when you are in the depths of your work.) You can't always give up every five minutes for your child. Maybe that would take away your shot of making a million dollars for your family. But it is still important to keep the end in mind. It's easy to forget why you started.

Your end pursuit should inform all of your decisions.

If your goal of making a million dollars is rooted in status, if you desire to prove your haters wrong, then always be on the lookout for other ways to elevate your status. If status is really important to you, it should inform your decisions.

When you know what really matters to you, the end goal should guide your decisions, rather than getting sucked into a rabbit hole of the means.

Find your end. Expose the value that exists at the core of your desire.

To fully embrace purpose, you must operate on a deeper level — you must operate for your deepest values.

You can pursue any means, but the truth of purpose comes out when you understand the why behind your pursuit.

When you are clear on the depth of your values, you can find ways to pursue purpose in anything and in everything. The next step is turning your surface values into deeper values. What really matters?

Again, look at the deeper values you have landed on, is this a means or an end? If your greatest value is the means, translate it to the end.

EVEN IF YOU ONLY GET THIS:

- People often get wrapped up in pursuing the means and lose sight of the end.

- Purpose is about pursuing the end, not the means.

CHAPTER 18

PURPOSE IS A DOUBLE EDGED SWORD.

MOST PEOPLE THINK THEY ARE READY FOR BATTLE.

I can't tell you how many people say, *"I know what I value, I'm ready to do big things in this world."*

Sometimes when they stay up at night and pray for purpose, they are actually praying for purpose conditioned on comfort. People want a big life calling, but they don't want life to be tough. They would rather just sit in bed and be living out purpose with minimal effort.

Purpose and comfort rarely coexist. Growth rarely lives within your comfort zone.

There is a big difference. Some people like the idea of taking a risk. Some like the idea of pursuing purpose, but when it comes down to making the choice, they would rather pursue a path that is easy. Oftentimes there is no easy path to purpose. Purpose requires you to get out there and make things happen.

How do you know when you're ready for purpose?
You're ready for purpose — your thing — when you've landed on your double edged sword. When you have your double edged sword, that's when you're ready

for battle.

Your Double Edged Sword is when your unique gift for the world is rooted in value and fear.

When your deepest value in this world is also connected to one of your deepest fears.

When you have arrived on your double edged sword, that is how you know you are ready for purpose, ready to *Find Your Thing*.

THE DOUBLE EDGED SWORD.

Your double edged sword connects both your greatest fear and your greatest value. If used right, the double edged sword is one of the greatest weapons. With a double edged sword, you can be unstoppable.

What is your double edged sword?

I always saw a double edged sword as a sword with two edges — one to fight with and one that could equally destroy you.
But there is good news. A double edged sword doesn't need to be a double ended sword. A double edged sword actually has two strong edges.

When your fear is used side by side with your value, you have the potential to be unstoppable.

For so long, all that I could see was a double ended sword. The very thing that I was good at could also destroy me. My deepest fears held me back. My desire for accomplishment also made me a slave to accomplishment. Your desire for significance also makes you a slave to significance. Finally, I realized your fear and values can be used together. Your biggest fear, if controlled, can be used as a place of power.

Maybe you're familiar with this concept. It's used in the Disney movie, Frozen. (The truth is I don't like movies, but I have watched Frozen.)

Elsa, the main character, starts out with a power that she cannot control. The very thing that is unique to her ends up destroying her and others. She becomes overwhelmed in trying to control it.

Change happens when instead of trying to fix her fear, she embraces her value — love. There are many examples of this concept outside of a Disney movie, but hey, who doesn't love Frozen? The fear will always exist, but when you allow it to give strength to your value, that's when the game changes.

What is your double edged sword?

FEARS DON'T GO AWAY — SO USE THEM TO YOUR ADVANTAGE.

You will always keep your fear. Questions in your identity like, *"Am I significant?"* will always be there. When you take moments of pain and use them to grow, your sword will become the sharpest.

Most people miss this. They get so excited that they found their unique value in the world, then quickly grow discouraged when they encounter a challenge.

You will continue to struggle. There, I said it. You must be aware that you will continue to struggle. You will help others through their pain but you are not exempt from the struggle yourself. In fact, most days you will have some type of struggle. Most days you will have some type of trigger that ignites internal pain. The sustainable power of purpose comes when you use your struggles as opportunities to sharpen your own value.

> *"If the ax is dull and its edge unsharpened, more strength is needed, but skill will bring success."*
>
> ECCLESIASTES 10:10

How can I help others if I still need help myself?
How can this be my purpose when I continue to come back to the struggle myself?
How can I bring about significance in others when I continue to question my own significance to this world?

The reason that you continue to struggle is the reason why you have the strength to help others.

You will encounter challenges. You will continue to come to a place of frustration and discouragement. And yet, this is the exact reason you are capable. As you continue to fight the uphill battle, remember these are the very battles that increase your capacity to impact others. You do not have to labor in vain.

Who better to help someone fight a battle, than one who has already been there?

Your struggle is the exact reason you will be able to continue to uniquely help those around you. As you continue to encounter challenges, you will develop the strength to grow yourself and others.

You do not need to rid yourself of all fear. (Although I will say, if you figure out how to do that, please let me know.) Strength is continuing to grow from your moments of fear and insecurity.

Use the moments of fear to further strengthen your purpose and strengthen your pursuit.

EVEN IF YOU ONLY GET THIS:

- Your fears will not go away. Use them to strengthen your purpose, rather than to distract you.

- Just like Elsa in the movie Frozen can choose to live from fear or love, you also get a choice.

- The power is when you focus on a double edged sword rather than a double ended sword.

- Your struggles are what continue to give you the power to fight for the suffering of others.

- Once you know your double edged sword, now you are ready for battle.

CHAPTER 19

PURPOSE IS A WHY, NOT A WHAT.

PURPOSE IS NOT A WHAT, IT'S A WHY.

At this point you should have your double edge sword - which is rooted in the thing that matters to you so much. Once you know what you care about, there are a few more litmus tests to go through to make sure we can *Find Your Thing*.

Here is something that might blow your mind:
Purpose is not about you. We call it "your purpose" or "your thing" when the truth is, it's not about you.
It's about others.
When you ask yourself, What is my thing? — that question is about you.

Your thing will finally become a thing when you embrace a pursuit for others.
Your thing will resonate with you when it's no longer your own, it's no longer about you.
Find a pursuit for others.

Good news. We don't really have to do much finding, it already exists.
You have a great reason why that stems from your values.

Purpose is beyond you. (At least in this book, purpose is beyond you.)
Purpose is beyond a thing. It's greater than you, and it's greater than a thing. It's a full fledged mission — a greater calling. While your purpose may be unique to

you, it's not about you.

Purpose is not a what, it's a why.

If you want to know if you're pursuing purpose — ask yourself — is my purpose conditioned to a thing?

Purpose is not an accomplishment.

Purpose is not something that is conditional to a situation or a circumstance.

Purpose is not a thing. It's not starting a thing, joining a thing or creating a thing.

It is easy to pursue a what. It is easy to condition your purpose to be a thing.

If I can just achieve [insert thing], then I will be living my life on purpose.

Thing = a job, a relationship, a status

Thing = something you want to start or create

Thing = whatever you have built up in your mind

Purpose is too big to be conditioned to a thing.

Purpose is a why.

It's a greater reason for being.

What thing have you been equating to purpose?

Don't let your purpose fall victim to only existing in one thing.

Purpose is too big to be one thing.

When your purpose is a pursuit, you can pursue it regardless of where you are, regardless of who you are with, and regardless of what you are doing.

To *Find Your Thing*, to live your thing, you must begin to pursue your why and pursue it in everything.

EVEN IF YOU ONLY GET THIS:

- Litmus Test: Is your purpose conditioned on one thing?

- Most people condition their purpose one thing. This is devastating when the one thing in your life changes.

- If your thing were to no longer exist, would you still have purpose?

- Purpose is not a what, it's a why. It is greater than one thing.

- Too often people think their purpose depends on their job, on their location, and on external circumstances.

- True purpose is a greater reason for being.

- Once you have a greater reason for being, then you are ready to choose a thing.

CHAPTER 20

PURPOSE IS NOT CONDITIONED ON CIRCUMSTANCES.

PURPOSE HAS NO PHYSICAL BOUNDS.

PURPOSE CAN'T BE LIMITED TO ONE PLACE; PURPOSE HAS NO BOUNDS.

To fight the battle and gain ground for your purpose, there are no limits to where that can exist.

You must choose to see it wherever you are, or you will not see it anywhere. If you want to know if you're pursuing purpose — ask yourself — is my purpose conditioned based on an external circumstance?

Do you know Victor Frankl? Thank goodness I had an influential mentor in my life that summarized a book for me on Victor Frankl that I probably would have never picked up because the cover didn't interest me. (Unfortunately it's hard to know which opportunities to judge by the cover and which are ultimately the best decisions of your life.)

My summary: Victor Frankl was a man in the middle of a Nazi concentration camp. Mind you, this is something Frankl could not control. He could not control the external, but he knew the one piece he could control was his internal—his mindset. No matter what happened around him, he was in control of his pursuit and in control of his values.

When you are living life on purpose, purpose has the opportunity to exist everywhere.

This is why your purpose cannot be conditioned to a thing.

Whether you live in Australia or Colorado ...
Whether you work in your current job or switch to a new job ...
Whether you are living in a jail cell or on the streets ...

Purpose still exists.
The way you pursue purpose might look different, but purpose does not leave you.

Often clients of mine are frustrated with their current job situation. They feel limited and want something greater. They want to do something more in line with their passion and purpose.
I tell my clients: Find a way to live out your purpose where you are now. Even if you're working at the worst job ever, if you want to live out your purpose somewhere else, then you first must figure out how to live it out where you are. Especially if you want to live out purpose in a bigger way, you must learn how to pursue it where you are.

At the end of my coaching program, I work with people on the dreams they want to create. We work on what they want to create today and what they want to create some day. After they get excited about seeing what they want to create, I then scale back and ask:
What if everything stayed the same?

If all of your external circumstances stayed the same — how could you still live out purpose? This is key. **If you can see how to live out purpose where you are, then you can see it anywhere.**

Yes, certain circumstances will allow you to make a bigger impact than others, but to make a big impact, you know know how to expand your purpose right where you are.

If you can live out purpose where you are, then you can live it out anywhere.

If you can't find purpose in the present — how will you ever find it somewhere else?

Curious why your purpose hasn't expanded? Maybe you should start living it out where you are and see what doors open for you.

EVEN IF YOU ONLY GET THIS:

- Litmus Test: Can you live out your purpose now?

- Most people have their purpose conditioned to start later in life.

- When I graduate ... when I retire ... after I have kids.

- When the clock turns 5p.m., when the weekend gets here ... when my next vacation comes.

CHAPTER 21

PURPOSE HAS NO TIME BOUNDS.

PURPOSE HAS NO TIME BOUNDS.

Show me how you are pursuing purpose today, and I'll show you your future.

We like to wait. We like to wait on circumstances, timing and conditions. If you want to know if you're pursuing purpose — ask yourself — am I pursuing purpose now or am I waiting?

Too often we wait. We limit purpose to start:

…This weekend

…On my next vacation

…In the summer

…When I graduate

…When I get married

…After we have kids

Waiting is rarely the answer. **If you want to live out purpose someday, then you have to start today. If you don't start today, there is no way to be sure you ever will.**

When I was in college, I used to say, *"When I'm older, I want to be generous with my money and resources."* Then it hit me. If I want to be generous *one* day, then I have to be generous *today*. It's that simple. The only way you can ensure that you will be generous in the future is to start now.

Getting in the habit of doing things is effective.
We exist in our default decision making. Most of the decisions we make on a day to day basis are already determined because we made them once and they quickly became a habit.

If you start to be generous, it becomes part of who you are. Soon you don't have to make the conscious decision.

This is important. Your default decision making, as noted earlier in the book, is powerful. Even just the realization that you are in a default mode should wake you up.

Your eating habits…
Your workout habits…
Your reading habits…

Any habit, and therefore any lack of a habit, is part of your default decision making. ***If you want to change something, you must do it consciously until it becomes part of your default decision making.***

One of the greatest switches in my life has been switching to working out six days a week. I no longer think about going to the gym. It no longer causes me any pain or additional work. I just go. I find a way to make it work.

The success has nothing to do with working out. The success is creating a habit that now exists no matter what.

Saving money is part of my default decision making. (In some cases this is good, in some cases this is bad.) I naturally will go for an option that saves money because it's ingrained in my beliefs and my previous decisions. (Yes, I once opted for an Uber pool to save $0.55, even though I was running late for the airport. It truly is a default decision to save money.)

To change something — you must do it consciously and repeatedly.

With that being said, purpose is conscious. It must start now if you want it to be ingrained in who you are and in what you do. The more you consciously pursue a value, the more it becomes part of who you are, and of what you say and do.

This isn't about habits, this is about your pursuit.

Your choices have already been made for you — your default decision making already exists. **Take control and decide what you want to pursue, and pursue it.**

Purpose starts now if you want to be living on purpose *one* day.
In fact, the more you pursue it, the more it expands. Four years ago I started swimming. Very poorly, I began to swim. Anyone that saw me likely thought I was drowning. Although I still consider myself a poor swimmer, I have people come up to me every couple of weeks and say, "*Wow, you're a really good swimmer. Did you swim in high school?*" So badly, I want to laugh at them because if only they knew how much I still feared the underwater flip turn.
The point is, I chose to pursue swimming, even when I was not confident in my abilities. Swimming even though I was horrible is the very thing that has increased my capacity to swim. **If you want to have a bigger purpose, start pursuing it now.**

When I'm 80, I'll be a kick ass swimmer because I started early. Purpose is no different. **People think they are supposed to wake up and just be there. Purpose expands daily if you pursue and expand it.**

EVEN IF YOU ONLY GET THIS:

- Litmus Test: Can you live out your purpose even when you don't feel like it?

- Most people claim they want a bigger purpose but aren't willing to put in the work it takes.

- Comfort is one of the unspoken areas people desire with purpose.

- Are you willing to live your purpose, even without comfort? If the answer is no, then you're not seeking purpose. You're seeking comfort.

> *Why it matters to Find Your Thing*
  Living out your thing doesn't erase comfort. If anything, it brings on more challenges. To be grounded in your purpose means that you are ready to live it out, even when life get uncomfortable.

CHAPTER 22

PURPOSE IS NOT CONDITIONED ON A FEELING.

PURPOSE ISN'T CONDITIONED ON A FEELING.

When you have purpose, it doesn't mean you have to feel a certain way.

Bigger challenges = bigger purpose.
Show me the challenges you have fought through, and I will show you the size of your purpose.

Some of us want bigger challenges, but aren't even willing to fight through the ones we have. Purpose does not get to be conditioned by comfort and security.

Some of you are still waiting for a thing.
You are thinking to yourself if I find a thing that I am passionate about, then I will go all out. I will do whatever it takes - I will take risks; I will put myself out there.

Too often our search for a thing is actually a search for comfort.

We think we are a risk takers, and we say we are risk takers, but sometimes we are just risk taker wannabes. I learned this concept from Kim McManus. She asked a crowd of people if they were risk takers. She got cheering and applause, only to respond by saying, most of us are not risk takers. We are simply wannabe risk takers.

Are you waiting for the right feeling before you pursue purpose?

CHAPTER 23

PURPOSE WILL LEAD YOU TO FIND YOUR THING.

PURSUE IT.

You have purpose, now you can pursue it.

It's that simple.

But wait, what's my thing?

What comes first, the chicken or the egg?

The thing will rarely come first.

Out of purpose, a thing is created. Now that you have purpose, the desire to impact others in a greater way, your thing will naturally come.

The greater value you pursue will determine your decisions. It will determine where you live, where you work, who you work with, who you live with and even who you love.

Most people start with:

"Should I…Start a blog? Start an organization? Travel the world? Stay here for work?"

Things are created when purpose is in action. Physical things and things the human eye cannot see. People look for circumstances to dictate purpose, and yet one's pursuit of purpose will dictate the circumstances.

Do not wait on one perfect thing before you take action.
(At least not if you are looking for sustainable fulfillment.)
Start with a reason for being, and then create the thing. You can create anything.

You now have a reason. (At least by now you should have a reason.)
Go pursue it.
Create something in line with your purpose and you cannot go wrong.

Once you put your value into the world, a thing will naturally be created.
Creating something is inevitable when you are pursuing a mission. Doing big
things is inevitable when you are living in line with the values that matter to you.

"I think I found my thing, but I'm not quite sure?"
This is what Samantha said to me when she first read the book. She recapped
for me that her deeper fear was not being connected, and her deepest fear was
that she didn't matter. After making the shift to flip the double edged sword,
Samantha said her deepest value was *mattering*.

Samantha has the ability to make people matter. She is a teacher. Making her
students matter is natural and happens daily. Samantha would also be described
by many as "one of the best friends known to man." Her *thing* is not being a
teacher, and her thing is not being a best friend to everyone. Samantha's greatest
gift is making *others* matter.

**Purpose is looking at her deeper value and seeing how she uniquely expresses
that value.** There are unique ways that Samantha makes other people feel like
they matter.
Samantha has the ability to press into people's lives. She can make anyone feel
cared for. When she moved in with her ninety-year old grandma, she made her
feel like she mattered. Every day she walks into her classroom, she makes her
students feel like they matter.

Purpose is seeing how uniquely your greatest value comes to life. There are
one million ways you can make someone feel like they matter. Samantha has a
unique way of doing this. When she sees her uniqueness of her greatest value,
then she can operate in purpose.

Now what should Samantha do? Does she need to switch careers? Does she need to start a blog? The truth is, it doesn't matter. She gets to choose. The way to bring satisfaction in her life is:

1. **Stay focused on the value.** Too often people slip back into fighting battles of fear. They never move past their internal pain. Samantha could easily say, "I don't feel like I matter today." She could easily pout and cry herself to sleep because the pain is real. Instead, choosing purpose over the fear will keep her grounded in satisfaction.

2. **Stay centered on pursuing the greatest value.** Samantha has unique ways of living out this value. It is a daily decision to find greater ways to pursue the value. The question when deciding her thing is which opportunities will allow her to live out her purpose in the greatest way, Samantha gets to define what it means to live out her purpose in the greatest way. To some people, greatest means to impact as many as possible. To others, greatest means to impact as many people in the deepest way as possible. Regardless of what it means to you, continue to test out your greatest values so that you can stay centered in what really matters.

When you stay grounded in your purpose, you will always find your way back to your thing.

ONE LAST THING...

THANK YOU FOR READING MY BOOK!

Feedback means the world to me. I love hearing your thoughts and need feedback to make the next book better.

Please leave me a helpful review on Amazon.

amzn. to/ 2znQ0Jh

THANK YOU SO MUCH!

Lisa Zelenak

NOTES

NOTES

NOTES

NOTES

NOTES

NOTES

NOTES

Made in the USA
Monee, IL
01 November 2019